D1559961

GUIDE TO THE UPANISHADS

The secret knowledge of the Veda is the seed which is evolved later on into the Vedanta. Its inner practice and discipline is a seed of the latter practice and discipline of Yoga.

UPANISHADS

The Upanishads are at once profound religious scriptures,
— for they are a record of the deepest spiritual experiences, —
documents of revelatory and intuitive philosophy of an inexhaustible light, power and largeness and, whether written in verse or
cadenced prose, spiritual poems of an absolute, an unfailing
inspiration inevitable in phrase, wonderful in rhythm and expression. It is the expression of a mind in which philosophy and
religion and poetry are made one, because this religion does not
end with a cult nor is limited to a religio-ethical aspiration, but
rises to an infinite discovery of God, of Self, of our highest and
whole reality of spirit and being and speaks out of an ecstasy of
luminous knowledge and an ecstasy of moved and fulfilled experience, this philosophy is not an abstract intellectual speculation
about Truth or a structure of the logical intelligence, but Truth
seen, felt, lived, held by the inmost mind and soul in the joy of
utterance of an assured discovery and possession, and this poetry
is the work of the aesthetic mind lifted up beyond its ordinary
field to express the wonder and beauty of the rarest spiritual
self-vision and the profoundest illumined truth of self and God
and universe. Here the intuitive mind and intimate psychological experience of the Vedic seers passes into a supreme culmination in which the Spirit, as is said in a phrase of the Katha
Upanishad, discloses its own very body, reveals the very word
of its self-expression and discovers to the mind the vibration of
rhythms which repeating themselves within in the spiritual
hearing seem to build up the soul and set it satisfied and complete on the heights of self-knowledge.

The Upanishads are Vedanta, a book of knowledge in a higher
degree even than the Vedas, but knowledge in the profounder
Indian sense of the word, *Jnāna*. Not a mere thinking and considering by the intelligence, the pursuit and grasping of a
mental form of truth by the intellectual mind, but a seeing of it
with the soul and a total living in it with the power of the inner
being, a spiritual seizing by a kind of identification with the
object of knowledge is *Jnāna*. And because it is only by an

integral knowing of the self that this kind of direct knowledge can be made complete, it was the self that the Vedantic sages sought to know, to live in and to be one with it by identity. And through this endeavour they came easily to see that the self in us is one with the universal self of all things and that this self again is the same as God and Brahman, a transcendent Being or Existence, and they beheld, felt, lived in the inmost truth of all things in the universe and the inmost truth of man's inner and outer existence by the light of this one and unifying vision. The Upanishads are epic hymns of self-knowledge and world-knowledge and God-knowledge.

The Upanishads abound with passages which are at once poetry and spiritual philosophy, of an absolute clarity and beauty, but no translation empty of the suggestions and the grave and subtle and luminous sense echoes of the original words and rhythms can give any idea of their power and perfection. There are others in which the subtlest psychological and philo-sopical truths are expressed with an entire sufficiency without falling short of a perfect beauty of poetical expression and always so as to live to the mind and soul and not merely be presented to the understanding intelligence. There is in some of the prose Upanishads another element of vivid narrative and tradition which restores for us though only in brief glimpses the picture of that extraordinary stir and movement of spiritual enquiry and passion for the highest knowledge which made the Upanishads possible. The scenes of the old world live before us in a few pages, the sages sitting in their groves ready to test and teach the comer, princes and learned Brahmins and great landed nobles going about in search of knowledge, the king's son in his chariot and the illegitimate son of the servant-girl, seeking any man who might carry in himself the thought of light and the word of revelation, the typical figures and personalities, Janaka and the subtle mind of Ajatashatru, Raikwa of the cart, Yajnavalkya militant for truth, calm and ironic, taking to himself with both hands without attachment worldly possessions and spiritual riches and casting at last all his wealth behind to wander forth as a houseless ascetic, Krishna, son of Devaki who heard a single word of the Rishi Ghora and knew at once the Eternal, the Ashramas, the courts of kings who were also spiritual discoverers and thinkers, the great sacrificial assemblies where the sages met and compared their knowledge. And we see how the soul of India was born and how arose this great birth-song in which it soared from its earth into the supreme empyrean of the spirit. The Vedas and the Upanishads are not only the sufficient fountain-head of Indian philosophy and religion, but of all Indian art, poetry and literature. It was the soul, the temperament, the ideal mind formed and expressed in them which later carved out the great philosophies, built the structure of the Dharma, recorded its heroic youth in the Mahabharata and Ramayana, intellectualised indefatigably in the classical times of the ripeness of its manhood, threw out so many original intuitions in science, created so rich a glow of aesthetic and vital and sensuous experience, renewed its spiritual and psychic experience in Tantra and Purana, flung itself into grandeur and beauty of line and colour, hewed and cast its thought and vision in stone and bronze, poured itself into new channels of self-expression in the later tongues and now after eclipse re-emerges always the same in difference and ready for a new life and a new creation.

GUIDE TO THE UPANISHADS

ABSOLUTE. In the Upanishads, in the inspired scripture of the most ancient Vedanta, we find the affirmation of the Absolute, the experience-concept of the utter and ineffable Transcendence; but we find also, not in contradiction to it but as its corollary, an affirmation of the cosmic Divinity, an experience-concept of the cosmic Self and the becoming of Brahman in the universe. Equally, we find the affirmation of the Divine Reality in the individual : this too is an experience-concept; it is seized upon not as an appearance, but as an actual becoming. In place of a sole supreme exclusive affirmation negating all else than the transcendent Absolute we find a comprehensive affirmation carried to its farthest conclusion : this concept of Reality envelops in one view the cosmic and the Absolute.

The Isha Upanishad insists on the unity and reality of all the manifestations of the Absolute; it refuses to confine truth to any one aspect. Brahman is the stable and the mobile, the internal and the external, all that is near and all that is far whether spiritually or in the extension of Time and Space ; it is the Being and all becomings, the Pure and Silent who is without feature or action and the Seer and Thinker who organises the world and its objects ; it is the One who becomes all that we are sensible of in the universe, the Immanent and that in which he takes up his dwelling. The Upanishad affirms the perfect and the liberating knowledge to be that which excludes neither the Self nor its creations ; the liberated spirit sees all these as becomings of the Self-existent in an internal vision and by a consciousness which perceives the universe within itself instead of looking out on it, like the limited and egoistic mind, as a thing other than itself. To live in the cosmic Ignorance is a blindness, but to confine oneself in an exclusive absolutism of Knowledge is also a blindness : to know Brahman as at once and together the Knowledge and the Ignorance, to attain to the supreme status at once by the Becoming and the

Non-Becoming, to relate together realisation of the transcendent and the cosmic self, to achieve foundation in the supramundane and a self-aware manifestation in the mundane, is the integral knowledge ; this is the possession of Immortality.

An Experience of the Absolute : There is only a timeless Eternal, a spaceless Infinite, the utterness of the Absolute, a nameless Peace, an overwhelming single objectless Ecstasy. There can be no denial of the overwhelming decisive convincingness — *ekātmya-pratyayasāram* — with which this realisation seizes the consciousness of the spiritual seeker.

ACTION. Freedom does not depend upon inaction, nor is this possession limited to the enjoyment of the inactive Soul that only witnesses without taking part in the movement. On the contrary, the doing of works in this material world and a full acceptance of the term of physical life are part of its completeness. For the active Brahman fulfils Itself in the world by works and man also is in the body for self-fulfilment by action. He cannot do otherwise, for even his inertia acts and produces effects in the cosmic movement. Being in this body or any kind of body, it is idle to think of refraining from action or escaping the physical life. The idea that this in itself can be a means of liberation, is part of the Ignorance which supposes the soul to be a separate entity in the Brahman.

Action is shunned because it is thought to be inconsistent with freedom. The man when he acts, is supposed to be necessarily entangled in the desire behind the action, in subjection to the formal energy that drives the action and in the results of the action. These things are true in appearance, not in reality.

Desire is only a mode of the emotional mind which by ignorance seeks its delight in the object of desire and not in the Brahman who expresses Himself in the object. By destroying that ignorance one can do action without entanglement in desire.

The Energy that drives is itself subject to the Lord, who expresses Himself in it with perfect freedom. By getting behind Nature to the Lord of Nature, merging the individual in the cosmic Will, one can act with the divine freedom. Our actions are given up to the Lord and our personal responsibility ceases in His liberty.

The chain of Karma only binds the movement of Nature and not the soul which, by knowing itself, ceases even to appear to be bound by the result of its works. Therefore the way of freedom is not inaction, but to cease from identifying oneself with the movement and recover instead our identity in the Self of things who is their Lord.

ADITI. " Aditi, the mother of the Gods, deep in the heart of things she has entered, there she is seated." (Katha Up., II. 1. 7)

AGNI. Agni is the heat and flame of the conscious force in Matter which has built up the universe ; it is he who has made life and mind possible and developed them in the material universe where he is the greatest deity. Especially he is the primary impeller of speech of which Vayu is the medium and Indra the lord. This heat of conscious force in Matter is *Agni Jātavedas*, the knower of all births ; of all things born, of every cosmic phenomenon he knows the law, the process, the limit, the relation.

ĀJNĀNA. The operation by which consciousness dwells on an image of things so as to govern and possess it in power.

Perception by receptive and central Will, implies a command from the brain.

AKSARA PURUṢA. The Self, standing back from the changes and movements of Nature, calm, pure, impartial, indifferent, watching them and not participating, above them as on a summit, not immersed in these Waters. This calm Self is the sky that never moves and changes looking down upon the waters that are never at rest. The *aksara* is the hidden freedom of the *ksara*.

ĀNANDA. Beatitude, the bliss of pure conscious existence and energy, as opposed to the life of the sensations and emotions which are at the mercy of the outward touches of Life and Matter and their positive and negative reactions, joy and grief, pleasure and pain. Ananda is the divine counterpart of the lower emotional and sensational being.

The essential nature of bliss of the cosmic consciousness and, in activity, its delight of self-creation and self-experience.

The Divine on the Ananda plane is not incapable of a world-play or self-debarred from any expression of its glories. On the contrary, as the Upanishad insists, the Ananda is the true creative principle. For all takes birth from this divine Bliss. Therefore the world of the Ananda is called the Janaloka, in the double sense of birth and delight.

ānanda ākāśa : Ether of bliss, the matrix and continent of the universal expression of the Self.

ānanda-brahma : " He knew Bliss for the Eternal. For from Bliss alone, it appears, are these creatures born and being born they live by Bliss and to Bliss they go hence and return." (Taittiriya Up., III. 6)

ānandamaya puruṣa : The Upanishad tells us that after the knowledge-self above the mental is possessed and all the lower selves have been drawn up into it, there is another and the last step of all still left to us—though one might ask, is it eternally the last or only the last practically conceivable or at all neces-sary for us now ?—to take up our gnostic existence into the Bliss-Self and there complete the spiritual self-discovery of the divine Infinite. Ananda, a supreme Bliss eternal, far other and higher in its character than the highest human joy or pleasure is the essential and original nature of the spirit. In Ananda our spirit will find its true self, in Ananda its essential cons-ciousness, in Ananda the absolute power of its existence. The embodied soul's entry into this highest absolute, unlimited, unconditional bliss of the spirit is the infinite liberation and the infinite perfection.

ānandamaya ātmā : " There is yet a second and inner Self which is other than this which is of Knowledge and it is fashioned out of Bliss. And the Self of Bliss fills the Self of Knowledge. Now the Bliss Self is made in the image of a man ; according as is the human image of the other, so is it made in the image of the man. Love is the head of him ; Joy is his right side ; pleasure is his left side ; Bliss is his spirit which

is the self of him ; the Eternal is his lower member wherein
he rests abidingly." (Taittiriya Up., II. 5)

"This Self of Bliss is the soul in the body to the former one
which was of Knowledge." (Taittiriya Up., II. 6)

Calculus of Ananda :   "Behold this exposition of the Bliss
to which ye shall hearken. Let there be a young man, excel-
lent and lovely in his youth, a great student ; let him have fair
manners, and a most firm heart and great strength of body,
and let all this wide earth be full of wealth for his enjoying.
That is the measure of bliss of one human being. Now a
hundred and a hundredfold of the human measure of bliss, is
the one bliss of men that have become angels in heaven. And
this is the bliss of the Vedawise whose soul the blight of desire
touches not. A hundred and a hundredfold of this measure of
angelic bliss is one bliss of Gods that are angels in heaven.
And this is the bliss of the Vedawise whose soul the blight of
desire touches not. A hundred and a hundredfold of this measure
of divine angelic bliss is one bliss of the Fathers whose world of
heaven is their world for ever. And this is the bliss of the Vedawise whose soul the blight of desire touches not. A hundred and
a hundredfold of this measure of bliss of the Fathers whose
worlds are for ever, is one bliss of the Gods who are born as
Gods in heaven. And this is the bliss of the Vedawise whose
soul the blight of desire touches not. A hundred and a hundredfold of this measure of bliss of the first-born in heaven, is one
bliss of the Gods of work who are Gods, for by the strength
of their deeds they depart and are Gods in heaven. And this
is the bliss of the Vedawise whose soul the blight of desire
touches not. A hundred and a hundredfold of this measure of
bliss of the Gods of work, is one bliss of the great Gods who
are Gods for ever. And this is the bliss of the Vedawise whose
soul the blight of desire touches not. A hundred and a hundredfold of this measure of divine bliss, is one bliss of Indra,
the King in Heaven. And this is the bliss of the Vedawise
whose soul the blight of desire touches not. A hundred and a
hundredfold of this measure of Indra's bliss is one bliss of
Brihaspati, who taught the Gods in heaven. And this is the
bliss of the Vedawise whose soul the blight of desire touches
not. A hundred and a hundredfold of this measure of Brihas-

pati's bliss, is one bliss of Prajapati, the Almighty Father. And this is the bliss of the Vedawise whose soul the blight of desire touches not. A hundred and a hundredfold of this measure of Prajapati's bliss, is one bliss of the Eternal Spirit. And this is the bliss of the Vedawise whose soul the blight of desire touches not. (Taittiriya Up., II. 8)

ANNAM. In its origin the word meant simply being or substance. In the Upanishads the physical substance is called *annam*, Food. For the dynamic energies of Prana feed upon physical substances.

" Food is the Eternal Father : for of this came the seed and of the seed is the world of creatures born." (Prashna Up., I. 14)

" Verily, man, this human being, is made of the essential substance of food." (Taittiriya Up., II. 1)

" From food all creatures are born and being born they grow by food. Lo, it is eaten and it eats ; yea, it devours the creatures that feed upon it, therefore it is called food from the eating." (Taittiriya Up., II. 2)

" Thou shalt not blame food ; for that is thy commandment unto labour." (Taittiriya Up., III. 7)

annam brahma : " He knew food for the Eternal. For from food alone, it appears, are these creatures born and being born they live by food, and into food they depart and enter again." (Taittiriya Up., III. 2)

annamaya puruṣa : Poised in the principle of Matter, the Spirit becomes the physical self of a physical universe in the reign of a physical Nature ; Spirit is then absorbed in its experience of Matter, it is dominated by the ignorance and inertia of the tamasic Power proper to physical existence. In the individual it becomes a materialised soul, *annamaya puruṣa,* whose life and mind have developed out of the ignorance and inertia of the material principle and are subject to their fundamental limitations. For life in Matter works in dependence on the body ; mind in Matter works in dependence on the body and on the vital or nervous being ; spirit itself in Matter is limited and divided in its self-relation and its power by the limitations and divisions of this matter-governed and life-driven mind. This materialised soul lives bound to the physical body and its narrow superficial external consciousness, and it takes normally the experiences of its physical organs, its senses, its matter-bound life and mind, with at most some limited spiritual glimpses, as the whole truth of existence.

Man is a spirit, but a spirit that lives as a mental being in physical Nature ; he is to his own self-consciousness a mind in a physical body. But at first is this mental being materialised and he takes the materialised soul, *annamaya purusa,* for his real self. He is obliged to accept, as the Upanishad expresses it, Matter for the Brahman because his vision here sees Matter as that from which all is born, by which all lives and to which all return in their passing. His natural highest concept of Spirit is an Infinite, preferably an inconscient Infinite, inhabiting or pervading the material universe (which alone it really knows), and manifesting by the power of its presence all these forms around him. His natural highest conception of himself is a vaguely conceived soul or spirit, a soul manifested only by the physical life's experiences, bound up with physical phenomena and forced on its dissolution to return by an automatic necessity to the vast indeterminateness of the Infinite.

APPEARANCES OF GOD. " In the self one sees God as in a mirror, but as in a dream in the world of the Fathers : and as in water one sees the surface of an object, so one sees Him in the world of the Gandharvas. But He is seen as light and shade in the heaven of the Spirit." (Katha Up., II. 3. 5)

APAS. Waters, otherwise called the seven streams or the seven fostering Cows, are the Vedic symbol for the seven cosmic principles and their activities, three inferior, the physical, vital and mental, four superior, the divine Truth, the divine Bliss, the divine Will and Consciousness, and the divine Being. On this conception also is founded the ancient idea of the seven worlds in each of which the seven principles are separately active by their various harmonies.

ARVAN. The strong one, the stallion or the bull, master of the herd, the leader, master or the fighter.
vāhana (vehicle) for the Asura, Titan.

ASURA. The Asuras are angels of might and force and violent struggle, self-will is their characteristic, just as an undisciplined fury of self-indulgence is the characteristic of their kindred Rakshasas. It is a self-will capable of discipline, but always huge and impetous, even in discipline, always based on a colossal egoism. They struggle gigantically to impose that egoism on their surroundings.

vāhana : It is for these mighty but imperfect beings that the Horse adapts himself to their needs (as *arvan*), becomes full of force and might and bears up their gigantic struggle, their increasing effort.

AŚVA. *aśva*, Horse, meant to the Rishis the unknown power made up of force, strength, solidity, speed and enjoyment that pervades and constitutes the material world.

vāhana for Man.

AŚVAMEDHA. The *aśvamedha* or Horse-Sacrifice is the symbol of a great spiritual advance, an evolutionary movement, almost from out of the dominion of apparently material forces into a higher spiritual freedom.

The Horse of the *aśvamedha* (in the Brhadāraṇyaka Up.) is a physical figure representing an unknown quantity of force and speed. This force, this speed is something world-wide, something universal ; it fills the regions with its being, it occupies Time, it gallops through Space, it bears on in its speed men and gods and the Titans. It is the Horse of the Worlds, and yet the Horse sacrificial.

AŚVATTHA TREE. Images the cosmic existence in the Vedanta. This tree of cosmic existence has no beginning and no end, in space or in time ; for it is eternal and imperishable. The real form of it cannot be perceived by us in this material world of man's embodiment, nor has it any apparent lasting foundation here ; it is an infinite movement and its foundation is above in the supreme of the Infinite. Its principle is the ancient sempiternal urge to action, *pravṛtti*, which for ever proceeds without beginning or end from the original Soul of all existence. Therefore its original source is above beyond

Time in the Eternal, but its branches stretch down below and it extends and plunges its other roots, well-fixed and clinging roots of attachment and desire with their consequences of more and more desire and endlessly developing action, plunges them downward here into the world of men. The branches of this cosmic tree extend both below and above, below in the material, above in the supraphysical planes.

" This is the eternal Tree with its root above and its branches downward ; this is Brahman, this is the Immortal ; in it are lodged all the worlds and none goes beyond it. This and That are one." (Katha Up., II. 3. 1)

ATMAN. Brahman is, subjectively, Atman, the Self or immutable existence of all that is in the universe.

Atman, our true self, is Brahman ; it is pure indivisible Being, self-luminous, self-concentrated in consciousness, self-concentrated in force, self-delighted. Its existence is light and bliss. It is timeless, spaceless and free.

Atman represents itself to the consciousness of the creature in three states, dependent on the relations between *purusa* and *prakṛti*, the Soul and Nature. These three states are *aksara* unmoving or immutable ; *kṣara*, moving or mutable ; and *para* or *uttama*, Supreme or Highest.

Atman, the Self, represents itself differently in the sevenfold movement of Nature according to the dominant principle of the consciousness in the individual being.

In the physical consciousness Atman becomes the material being, *annamaya purusa.*

In the vital or nervous consciousness Atman becomes the vital or dynamic being, *prānamaya purusa.*

In the mental consciousness Atman becomes the mental being, *manomaya purusa.*

In the supra-intellectual consciousness, dominated by the Truth or causal Idea, Atman becomes the ideal being or great Soul, *vijñānamaya purusa* or *mahat ātman.*

In the consciousness proper to the universal Beatitude, Atman becomes the all-blissful being or all-enjoying and all-productive Soul, *ānandamaya purusa.*

In the consciousness proper to the infinite divine self-awareness which is also the infinite all-effective Will, Atman is the
all-conscious Soul that is source and lord of the universe,
caitanya puruṣa.

In the consciousness proper to the state of pure divine existence Atman is *sat purusa,* the pure divine Self.

Vide Self.

ATTAINMENT. "Attaining to him, seers glad with fullness of knowledge, perfected in the self, all passions cast from
them, tranquillised,—these, the wise, come to the all-pervading
from every side, and, uniting themselves with him enter utterly
the All. Doers of askesis who have made sure of the aim of
the whole knowledge of Vedanta, the inner being purified by the
Yoga of renunciation, all in the hour of their last end passing
beyond death are released into the worlds of the Brahman."
(Mundaka Up., III. 2. 5-6)

"As rivers in their flowing reach their home in the ocean
and cast off their names and forms, even so one who knows is
delivered from name and form and reaches the Supreme beyond
the Most High, even the Divine Person." (Mundaka Up.,
III. 2. 8)

Conditions of Attainment. "None who has not ceased from
doing evil, or who is not calm, or not concentrated in his being,
or whose mind has not been tranquillised, can by wisdom attain
to Him." (Katha Up., I. 2. 24)

AUM AND CONCENTRATION. In all Yoga there are
indeed many preparatory objects of thought-concentration,
forms, verbal formulas of thought, significant names, all of
which are supports to the mind in this movement, all of which
have to be used and transcended ; the highest support according to the Upanishads is the mystic syllable AUM, whose three
letters represent the Brahman or Supreme Self in its three
degrees of status, the Waking Soul, the Dream Soul and the
Sleep Soul, and the whole potent sound rises towards that which
is beyond status as beyond activity. For all Yoga of knowledge
the final goal is the Transcendent.

Vide Om.

BECOMING. The totality of objects (*arthān*) is the becoming of the Lord in the extension of His own being. Its principle is double. There is consciousness; there is Being. Consciousness dwells in energy (*tapas*) upon its self-being to produce Idea of itself (*vijnāna*) and form and action inevitably corresponding to the Idea. This is the original Indian conception of creation, self-production or projection into form (*srṣṭi, prasava*). Being uses its self-awareness to evolve infinite forms of itself governed by the expansion of the innate Idea in the form. This is the original Indian conception of evolution, prominent in certain philosophies such as the Sankhya (*parināma, vikāra, vivarta*). It is the same phenomenon diversely stated.

In the idea of some thinkers the world is a purely subjective evolution (*vivarta*), not real as objective facts; in the idea of others it is an objective fact, a real modification (*parināma*), but one which makes no difference to the essence of Bueig. Both notions claim to derive from the Upanishads as their authority, and their opposition comes in fact by the separation of what in the ancient Vedanta was viewed as one, — as we see in this passage.

Brahman is his own subject and his own object, whether in His pure self-existence or in His varied self-becoming. He is the object of His own self-awareness; He is the Knower of His own self-being. The two aspects are inseparable, even though they seem to disappear into each other and emerge again from each other. All appearance of pure subjectivity holds itself as an object implicit in its very subjectivity; all appearance of pure objectivity holds itself as subject implicit in its very objectivity.

All objective existence is the Self-existent, the Self-becoming, *svayambhū*, becoming by the force of the Idea within it. The Idea is, self-contained, the Fact that it becomes. For *svayambhū* sees or comprehends Himself in the essence of the Fact as *kavi*, thinks Himself out in the evolution of its possibilities as *manīṣi*, becomes form of Himself in the movement in Space and Time as *paribhū*. These three are one operation appearing as successive in the relative, temporal and spatial Consciousness.

BEING AND BECOMING. Being and Becoming, One and Many are both true and are both the same thing : Being is one, Becomings are many ; but this simply means that all Becomings are one Being who places Himself variously in the phenomenal movement of His consciousness.

BELIEF. We must believe in God before we can know him ; we must realise him as the " HE is " before we realise him in his essential.

BEYOND. " It is other than the known, and it is above and beyond the unknown." (Kena Up., I, 3).
" There the sun cannot shine and and the moon has no lustre : all the stars are blind : there our lightnings flash not, neither any earthly fire. For all that is bright is but the shadow of His brightness and by His shining all this shines." (Katha Up. II, 2. 15).
" There the sun shines not and the moon has not splendour and the stars are blind ; there these lightnings flash not, how then shall burn this earthly fire ? All that shines is but the shadow of his shining ; all this universe is effulgent with his light." (Mundaka Up. II, 2. 11).

BHRIGU'S SEEKINGS FOR THE REALITY. First he found the ultimate reality to be Matter and the physical, the material being, the external man our only self and spirit. Next he fixed on life as the Reality and the vital being as the self and spirit ; in the third essay on Mind and the mental being ; only afterwards could he get beyond the superficial subjective through the supramental Truth consciousness to the eternal, the blissful, the ever creative Reality of which these are the sheaths.

BIRTH AND NON-BIRTH. The reason for this double movement is that we are intended to realise immortality in the Birth. The self is uniform and undying and in itself always possesses immortality. It does not need to descend into Avidya and Birth to get that immortality of Non-Birth ; for it possesses it always. It descends in order to realise and possess it as the individual Brahman in the play of world-existence. It accepts

Birth and Death, assumes the ego and then dissolving the ego by the recovery of unity realises itself the Lord, the One, and Birth as only a becoming of the Lord in mental and formal being : this becoming is now governed by the true sight of the Seer and, once this is done, becoming is no longer inconsistent with Being, birth becomes a means and not an obstacle to the enjoyment of immortality by the lord of this formal habitation. This is our proper course and not to remain for ever in the chain of birth and death, nor to flee from birth into a pure non-becoming. The bondage does not consist in the physical act of becoming, but in the persistance of the ignorant sense of the separate ego. The Mind creates the chain and not the body.

" Into a blind darkness they enter who follow after the Non-Birth, they as if into a greater darkness who devote themselves to the Birth alone. He who knows That as both in one, the Birth and the dissolution of Birth, by the dissolution crosses beyond death and by the Birth enjoys Immortality." (Isha Up. 12, 14).

BIRTHS. " There is a birth and growth of the self. According to his actions the embodied being assumes forms successively in many places ; many forms gross and subtle he assumes by force of his own qualities of nature." (Shvetashva-tara Up. V. 11, 12).

BLIND LEADING BLIND. " They who dwell in the ignorance, within it, wise in their own wit and deeming themselves very learned, men bewildered are they who wander about stumbling round and round helplessly like blind men led by the blind." (Katha Up. I. 2. 5).

" They who dwell shut within the ignorance and they hold themselves for learned men thinking ' We, even we are the wise and the sages ' — fools are they and they wander around beaten and stumbling like blind men led by the blind." (Mundaka Up. I. 2. 8).

BLISS. A transcendent Bliss, unimaginable and inexpressible by the mind and speech, is the nature of the Ineffable.

That broods immanent and secret in the whole universe and in everything in the universe. Its presence is described as a secret ether of the bliss of being of which the Scripture says that, if this were not, none could for a moment breathe or live. And this spiritual bliss is here also in our hearts.

Vide **Ananda.**

"Who could labour to draw in the breath or who could have strength to breathe it out, if there were not that Bliss in the heaven of his heart, the ether within his being? It is He that is the fountain of bliss." (Taittiriya. Up. II. 7).

BODY AND LIFE. "The Breath of things is an immortal Life but of this body ashes are the end." (Isha Up. 17).

BRAHMALOKA. Some supreme self-expression of the Being as Spirit in which the soul liberated into its highest perfection possesses the infinity and beatitude of the eternal Godhead.

BRAHMAN. Whatever reality is in existence, by which all the rest subsists, that is Brahman. An Eternal behind all instabilities, a Truth of things which is implied, if it is hidden in all appearances, a Constant which supports all mutations, but is not increased, diminished, abrogated, — there is such an unknown x which makes existence a problem, our own self a mystery, the universe a riddle. If we were only what we seem to be to our normal self-awareness, there would be no mystery; if the world were only what it can be made out to be by the perception of the senses and their strict analysis in the reason, there would be no riddle; and if to take our life as it is now and the world as it has so far developed to our experience were the whole possibility of our knowing and doing, there would be no problem. Or at best there would be but a shallow mystery, an easily solved riddle, the problem only of a child's puzzle. But there is more, and that more is the hidden head of the Infinite and the secret heart of the Eternal. It is the highest and this highest is the all; there is none beyond and there is none other than it. To know it is to know the highest and by knowing the highest to know all. For as it is the beginning and source of all things, so everything else is its consequence ; as it is the support and constituent of all things, so the secret of everything else is explained by its secret ; as it is the sum and end of all things, so everything else amounts to it and by throwing itself into it achieves the sense of its own existence.

This is the Brahman.

The Supreme Brahman is that which in Western metaphysics is called the Absolute : but Brahman is at the same time the omnipresent Reality in which all that is relative exists as its forms or its movements ; this is an Absolute which takes all relativities in its embrace. The Upanishads affirm that all this is the Brahman ; Mind is Brahman, Life is Brahman, Matter is Brahman ; addressing Vayu, the Lord of Air, of Life, it is said " O Vayu, thou art manifest Brahman " ; and, pointing to man and beast and bird and insect, each separately is identified with the One, — " O Brahman, thou art this old man and boy and girl, this bird, this insect." Brahman is the Consciousness that knows itself in all that exists ; Brahman is the Force that sustains the power of God and Titan and Demon, the Force that acts in man and animal and the forms and energies of Nature ; Brahman is the Ananda, the secret Bliss of existence which is the ether of our being and without which none could breathe or live. Brahman is the inner Soul in all ; it has taken a form in correspondence with each created form which it inhabits. The Lord of Beings is that which is conscious in the conscious being, but he is also the Conscious in inconscient things, the One who is master and in control of the many that are passive in the hands of Force-Nature. He is the Timeless and Time ; He is Space and all that is in Space ; He is Causality and the cause and the effect : He is the thinker and his thought, the warrior and his courage, the gambler and his dice-throw. All realities and all aspects and all semblances are the Brahman ; Brahman is the Absolute, the Transcendent and incommunicable, the Supracosmic Existence that sustains the cosmos, the Cosmic Self that upholds all beings, but It is too the self of each individual : the soul or psychic entity is an eternal portion of the Ishwara ; it is his supreme Nature or Consciousness-Force that has become the living being in a world of living beings. The Brahman alone is, and because of it all are, for all are the Brahman; this Reality is the reality of everything that we see in Self and Nature. Brahman, the Ishwara, is all this by his Yoga-Maya, by the power of his Consciousness-Force put out in self-manifestation: he is the Conscious Being, Soul, Spirit, Purusha, and it is by his Nature, the force of his conscious self-existence that he is all things; he is the Ishwara, the omniscient and omnipotent All-ruler, and it is by his Shakti, his conscious Power, that he manifests himself in Time and governs the universe.

Brahman in itself is unknowable and therefore beyond description. It is unknowable, not because it is a void and capable of no description except that of nothingness, nor — because, although positive in existence, it has no content or quality, but because it is beyond all things that our knowledge can conceive and because the methods of ideation and expression proper to our mentality do not apply to it. It is the absolute of all things that we know and of each thing that we know and yet nothing nor any sum of things can exhaust or characterise its essential being. For its manner of being is other than that which we call existence; its unity resists all analysis, its multiple infinities exceed every synthesis.

ānandam brahma : Brahman as the self-existent bliss and its universal delight of being.

anantam brahma : Brahman infinite in being and infinite in quality.

jnānam brahma : Brahman as self-existent consciousness and universal knowledge.

sarvam brahma : Brahman that is the All.

Brahman, Active and Inactive : The Inactive and the Active Brahman are simply two aspects of the one Self, the one Brahman who is the Lord. It is He who has gone abroad in the movement. He maintains Himself free from all modifications in His inactive existence. The inaction is the basis of the action and exists in the action; it is His freedom from all He does and becomes and in all He does and becomes. These are the positive and negative poles of one indivisible consciousness.

Brahman—Dual Status : Brahman is both the mobile and the immobile, i.e., the One and the Many, is the Self and all existences, *atmān, sarva bhūtāni*, is the Knowledge and the Igno-

rance, is the eternal unborn status and also the birth of
existences ; to dwell only on one part of these things to the
rejection of its eternal counterpart is a darkness of exclusive
knowledge or a darkness of ignorance. Man must know and
must embrace both and learn of the Supreme in his entirety in
order to enjoy immortality and live in the Eternal.

Brahman—Five conditions :   Brahman *Virāṭ*, Master of the
Waking Universe ; Brahman *Hiraṇya-Garbha*, of the Dream
Universe ; Brahman *Prājna* or *Avyakta*, of the Trance Universe
of Unmanifestation ; *Parabrahman*, the Highest ; and that which
is higher than the highest, the Unknowable.

Brahman and the Universe :   All this is the Eternal, all this is
the perennial self-seeing of the Self. *sarvam khalu idam brahma,
ayam ātmā brahma.*   The Eternal has become all existences,
ātmā abhūt sarvabhūtani as the Śvetāśvatara puts it, " Thou art
this boy and yonder girl and that old man walking supported on
his staff."

" All this is Brahman immortal, naught else ; Brahman is in
front of us, Brahman behind us, and to the south of us and to
the north of us and below us and above us ; it stretches everywhere. All this is Brahman alone, all this magnificent universe."
(Mundaka Up. II. 2. 12).

" Manifested, it is here set close within, moving in the secret
heart, this is the mighty foundation and into it is consigned all
that moves and breathes and sees. This that is that great
foundation here, know, as the Is and Is-not, the supremely
desirable, greatest and the Most High, beyond the knowledge
of creatures. That which is the luminous, that which is smaller
than the atoms, that in which are set the worlds and their
peoples, That is This, — it is Brahman immutable : life is That,
it is speech and mind. That is This, the True and Real, it is
That which is immortal : it is into That that thou must pierce,
O fair son, into That penetrate." (Mundaka Up. II. 2. I.2).

" Seek thou to know that from which these creatures are born,
whereby being born they live and to which they go hence and
enter again ; for that is the Eternal." (Traittiriya Up. III. 1).

Brahman and World :   The Upanishads do not deny the
reality of the world, but they identify it with Brahman who
transcends it. He is one without a second ; He is the All.   If

all is Brahman, then there can be nothing but Brahman, and therefore the existence of the All, *sarvam idam*, does not contradict the unity of Brahman, does not establish the reality of *bheda*, difference. It is one Intelligence looking at itself from a hundred view-points, each point conscious of and enjoying the existence of the others. The shoreless stream of idea and thought, imagination and experience, name and form, sensation and vibration sweeps onward for ever, without beginning, without end, rising into view, sinking out of sight ; through it the one Intelligence with its million self-expressions pours itself abroad, an ocean with innumerable waves. One particular self-expression may disappear into its source and continent, but that does not and cannot abolish the phenomenal universe. The One is for ever, and the Many are for ever because the One is for ever. So long as there is a sea, there will be waves.

Brahman in golden sheath :   " In a supreme golden sheath the Brahman lies, stainless, without parts. A Splendour is That, It is the Light of Lights, It is That which the self-knowers know." (Mundaka Up., II. 2. 10)

BRAHMAN-ATTAINMENT. The attainment of the Brahman is our escape from the mortal status into Immortality, by which we understand not the survival of death, but the finding of our true self of eternal being and bliss beyond the dual symbols of birth and death. By immortality we mean the absolute life of the soul as opposed to the transient and mutable life in the body which it assumes by birth and death and rebirth and superior also to its life as the mere mental being who dwells in the world subjected helplessly to this law of death and birth or seems at least by his ignorance to be subjected to this and to other laws of the lower Nature. To know and possess its true nature, free, absolute, master of itself and its embodiments is the soul's means of transcendence, and to know and possess this is to know and possess the Brahman. It is also to rise out of mortal world into immortal world, out of world of bondage into world of largeness, out of finite world into infinite world. It is to ascend out of earthly joy and sorrow into a transcendent Beatitude.

This must be done by the abandonment of our attachment to
the figure of things in the mortal world. We must put from us
its death and dualities if we would compass the unity and
immortality. Therefore it follows that we must cease to make
the goods of this world or even its right, light and beauty our
object of pursuit ; we must go beyond these to a supreme Good,
a transcendent Truth, Light and Beauty in which the opposite
figures of what we call evil disappear. But still, being in this
world, it is only through something in this world itself that we
can transcend it ; it is through its figures that we must find the
absolute.

BRAHMAN-CONSCIOUSNESS.   The Eternal outlook of the
Absolute upon the relative.

The Brahman-consciousness of which the Upanishad speaks is
not the Absolute withdrawn into itself, but that Absolute in
its outlook on the relative ; it is the Lord, the Master-Soul, the
governing Transcendent and All, He who constitutes and controls the action of the gods on the different planes of our being.

BRAHMAN-DELIGHT.   Our highest state of being is indeed
a becoming one with Brahman in his eternity and infinity,
but it is also an association with him in delight of self-
fulfilment, *aśunte saha brahmaṇā*. And that principle of the
Eternal by which this association is possible, is the principle of
his knowledge, his self-discernment, the wisdom by which he
knows himself perfectly in all the world and all beings,
brahmaṇā vipaścitā.

" The name of That is ' That Delight ' ; as That Delight one
should follow after It.   He who so knows That, towards him
verily, all existences yearn." (Kena Up., IV. 6)

BRAHMAN-KNOWER.   The knower of the Brahman sees
all these lower things in the light of the Highest, the external
and superficial as a translation of the internal and essential,
the finite from the view of the Infinite. He begins to see and
know existence no longer as the thinking animal, but as the
Eternal sees and knows it. Therefore he is glad and rich in
being, luminous in joy, satisfied of existence.

The knower of Brahman has not only the joy of light, but gains something immense as the result of his knowledge, *brahmavid āpnoti.*

What he gains is that highest, that which is supreme ; he gains the highest being, the highest consciousness, the highest wideness and power of being, the highest delight ; *brahmavid āpnoti param.*

" The knower of Brahman attains the Highest ; for this is the verse that was declared of old, ' Brahman is Truth, Brahman is Knowledge, Brahman is the Infinite, he finds Him hidden in the cavern heart of being ; in the highest heaven of His creatures, lo, he enjoys all desire and he abides with the Eternal, ever with that cognisant and understanding Spirit '." (Taittiriya Up., II. 1)

" He, verily, who knows that Supreme Brahman becomes himself Brahman ; in his lineage none is born who knows not the Brahman. He crosses beyond sorrow, he crosses beyond sin, he is delivered from the knotted cord of the secret heart and becomes immortal." (Mundaka Up., III. 2. 9)

BRAHMAN KNOWLEDGE. The Eternal is knowable, He defines himself so that we may seize him, and man can become, even while he exists as man and in this world and in this body, a knower of the Brahman.

" Of this knowledge austerity and self-conquest and works are the foundation, the Vedas are all its limbs, truth is its dwelling-place.

He who knows this knowledge, smites evil away from him and in that vaster world and infinite heaven finds his foundation, yea, he finds his foundation." (Kena Up., IV. 8, 9)

BRAHMAN-SELF FOURFOLD. Brahman as Self is fourfold ; the Self is Brahman and all that is is the Brahman, but all that is is the Self seen by the Self in four states of its being. In the pure self-status neither consciousness nor unconsciousness as we conceive it can be affirmed about Brahman ; it is a state of superconscience absorbed in its self-existence, in a self-silence or a self-ecstasy, or else it is the status of a free Superconscient containing or basing everything but involved in

nothing. But there is also a luminous status of sleep-self, a
massed consciousness which is the origin of cosmic existence ; this
state of deep sleep in which yet there is the presence of an omnipotent Intelligence is the seed state or causal condition from which
emerges the cosmos ; the dream-self which is the continent of all
subtle, subjective or supraphysical experience ; and the self of
waking which is the support of all physical experience.

BRAHMAN-VISION. We have to perceive Brahman comprehensively as both the Stable and the Moving. We must see
It in eternal and immutable Spirit and in all the changing
manifestation of universe and relativity.

We have to perceive all things in Space and Time, the far
and the near, the immemorial Past, the immediate Present, the
infinite Future with all their contents and happenings as the
One Brahman.

We have to perceive Brahman as that which exceeds, contains
and supports all individual things as well as all universe,
transcendentally of Time and Space and Causality. We have
to perceive It also as that which lives in and possesses the
universe and all it contains.

This is the transcendent, universal and individual Brahman,
Lord, Continent and Indwelling Spirit, which is the object of
all knowledge. Its realisation is the condition of perfection and
the way of Immortality.

BRAHMAVIDYĀ. " The highest knowledge of Brahman,
the secret knowledge ever followed by saints, how the wise man
swiftly putting from him all evil goeth to the Purusha who is
higher than the highest." (Kaivalya Up., 1)

This knowledge is the best or highest, because it goes beyond
the triple Brahman to the Purushottama or Most High God ;
it is secret, because even in the ordinary teaching of Vedanta,
Purana and Tantra, it is not expressed, it is always followed by
the saints, the initiates. The saints are those who are pure of
desire and full of knowledge and it is to these that the secret
knowledge has been given from the beginning. The substance
of the knowledge is how, by what means, one by knowledge can
swiftly put sin from him and reach Purushottama.

BREATH. " Man that is mortal lives not by the breath, no, nor by the lower breath ; but by something else we live in which both these have their being." (Katha Up., II. 2. 5)

Five Breaths. In the anus and in the organ of pleasure is the lower breath, and the eyes and the ears, the mouth and the nose, the main breath itself is seated ; but the medial breath is in the middle. This is he that equally distributes the burnt offering of food : for from this are the seven fires born. The Spirit in the heart abides, and in the heart there are one hundred and one nerves, and each nerve has a hundred branch-nerves and each branch-nerve has seventytwo thousand sub-branch-nerves : through these the breath pervasor moves. Of these many there is one by which the upper breath departs, that by virtue takes to the heaven of virtue, by sin to the hell of sin, and by mingled sin and righteousness back to the world of men restores. The Sun is the main breath outside this body, for it cherishes the eye in its rising. The divinity in the earth, she attracts the lower breath of man, and the ether between is the medial breath ; air is the breath pervasor. (Prashna Up., III. 5-8)

Vide Prana.

BRIDGE TO IMMORTALITY. " He in whom are inwoven heaven and earth and the mid-region, and mind with all the life-currents, Him know to be the one Self ; other words put away from you : this is the bridge to immortality. Where the nerves are brought close together like the spokes in the nave of a chariot-wheel, this is He that moves within,—there is He manifoldly born. Meditate on the Self as OM and happy be your passage to the other shore beyond the darkness. The Omniscient, the All-wise, whose is this might and majesty upon the earth, is this self-enthroned in the Divine city of the Brahman, in his ethereal heaven." (Mundaka Up., II. 2. 5-7)

CAITYA PURUṢA. The true soul secret in us—subliminal, we have said, but the word is misleading, for this presence is not situated below the threshold of waking mind, but rather burns in the temple of the inmost heart behind the thick screen of an ignorant mind, life and body, not subliminal but behind the veil,—this veiled psychic entity is the flame of the Godhead always alight within us, inextinguishable even by that dense unconsciousness of any spiritual self within which obscures our outward nature. It is a flame born out of the Divine and, luminous inhabitant of the Ignorance, grows in it till it is able to turn it towards the Knowledge. It is the concealed Witness and Control, the hidden guide, the Daemon of Socrates, the inner light or inner voice of the mystic. It is that which endures and is imperishable in us from birth to birth, untouched by death, decay or corruption, an indestructible spark of the Divine. Not the unborn Self or Atman, for the Self even in presiding over the existence of the individual is aware always of its universality and transcendence, it is yet its deputy in the forms of Nature, the individual soul, *caitya puruṣa*, supporting mind, life and body, standing behind the mental, the vital, the subtle-physical being in us and watching and profiting by their development and experience.

CHARACTER OF THE UPANISHADS. These supreme and all-embracing truths, these visions of oneness and self and a universal divine being are cast into brief and monumental phrases which bring them at once before the soul's eye and make them real and imperative to its aspiration and experience or are couched in poetic sentences full of revealing power and suggestive thought-colour that discover a whole infinite through a finite image. The One is there revealed, but also disclosed the many aspects, and each is given its whole significance by the amplitude of the expression and finds as if in a spontaneous self-discovery its place and its connection by the illumining justness of each word and all the phrase. The largest metaphysical truths and the subtlest subtleties of psychological experience are taken up into the inspired movement and made at once precise to the seeing mind and loaded with unending suggestion to the discovering spirit. There are separate phrases, single couplets, brief passages which contain each in itself the substance of a vast philosophy and yet each is only thrown out as a side, an aspect, a portion of the infinite self-knowledge. All here is a packed and pregnant and yet perfectly lucid and luminous brevity and an immeasurable completeness. A thought of this kind cannot follow the tardy, careful and diffuse development of the logical intelligence. The passage, the sentence, the couplet, the line, even the half line follows the one that precedes with a certain interval full of an unexpressed thought, an echoing silence between them, a thought which is carried in the total suggestion and implied in the step itself, but which the mind is left to work for its own profit, and these intervals of pregnant silence are large, the steps of this thought are like the paces of a Titan striding from rock to distant rock across infinite waters. There is a perfect totality, a comprehensive connection of harmonious parts in the structure of each Upanishad ; but it is done in the way of a mind that sees masses of truth at a time and stops to bring only the needed word out of a filled silence. The rhythm in verse or cadenced prose corresponds to the sculpture of the thought and the phrase. The metrical forms of the Upanishads are made up of four half lines each clearly cut, the lines mostly complete in themselves and integral in sense, the half line presenting two thoughts or distinct parts of a thought that are wedded to and complete each other, and the sound movement follows a corresponding principle, each step brief and marked off by the distinctness of its pause, full of echoing cadences that remain long vibrating in the inner hearing : each is as if a wave of the infinite that carries in it the whole voice and rumour of the ocean. It is a kind of poetry, — word of vision, rhythm of the spirit, — that has not been written before or after.

CHHANDOGYA UPANISHAD. Its subject is Brahman, but the Brahman as symbolised in the Om, the sacred syllable of the Veda ; not, therefore, the pure state of the universal existence, but that Existence in all its parts, the waking world and dream self and the sleeping, the manifest, half-manifest and hidden, *bhūrloka*, *bhuvar* and *svar*, — the right means to win all of them, enjoy all of them, transcend all of them.

Om, the syllable, technically called Udgitha, is to be meditated on as a symbol of the four-fold Brahman with two objectives, the " singing to " one's desires and aspirations in the triple manifestation and the spiritual ascension into the Brahman Itself so as to meet and enter into heaven after heaven and even into its Transcendent felicity. For, the Upanishad says, with the syllable Om one begins the chant of the *sāmaveda*, or, in the esoteric sense, by means of the meditation on Om one makes this soul-ascension and becomes master of all the soul desires.

To explain Brahman in Its nature and workings, to teach the right worship and meditation on Brahman to establish what are the different means of attainment of different results and the formulae of the meditation and worship, is its purpose. All this work of explanation has to be done in reference to the Veda and Vedic Sacrifice and ritual of which Om is the substance. In a certain sense, therefore, the Upanishad is an explanation of the purpose and symbology of Vedic formulae and ritual ; it sums up the results of the long travel of seeking by which the first founders and pioneers of Vedantism in an age when the secret and true sense of Veda had been largely submerged in the ceremonialism and formalism of the close of the Dwapara Yuga, attempted to recover their lost heritage partly by reference to the adepts who still remained in possession of it, partly by the tradition of the great seekers of the past *Yuga*, Janaka, Yajnavalkya, Krishna and others, partly by their own illuminations and spiritual experience. The Chhandogya Upanishad is thus the summary history of one of the greatest and most interesting ages of human thought.

CIT SAKTI. It is the supreme Energy (Tapas or Chit-Shakti) which is nothing but the infinite force in action of the supreme conscious Being in His own illumined self. The Self-existent is luminously aware of Himself and full of His own delight ; and that self-awareness is a timeless self-possession which in action reveals itself as a force of infinite consciousness omnipotent as well as omniscient ; for it exists between two poles, one of eternal stillness and pure identity, the other of eternal energy and identity of All with itself, the stillness eternally supporting the energy. That is the true existence, the Life from which our life proceeds.

Consciousness-force, inherent conscious force of conscious-being, which manifests itself as nervous energy full of sub-mental sensation in the plant, as desire-sense and desire-will in the primary animal forms, as self-conscious sense and force in the developing animal, as mental will and knowledge topping all the rest in man.

CIT-TAPAS. Pure energy of Consciousness, free in its rest or its action, sovereign in its will, as opposed to the hampered dynamic energies of Prana which, feeding upon physical substances, are dependent on and limited by their sustenance. Tapas is the divine counterpart of this lower nervous or vital energy.

CITY OF ELEVEN GATES. " The unborn who is not devious-minded has a city with eleven gates : when he takes up his abode in it, he grieves not, but when he is set free from it, that is his deliverance." (Katha Up. II. 2. 1).

COMMANDMENT TO THE DISCIPLE. " Speak truth, walk in the way of thy duty, neglect not the study of Veda. When thou hast brought to thy Master the wealth that he desires, thou shalt not cut short the long thread of thy race. Thou shalt not be negligent of truth ; thou shalt not be negligent of thy duty, thou shalt not be negligent of welfare ; thou shalt not be negligent towards thy increase and thy thriving ; thou shalt not be negligent of the study and teaching of Veda. Thou shalt not be negligent of thy work unto the Gods or thy works unto the Fathers. Let thy father be unto thee as thy God and thy mother as thy Goddess whom thou adorest. Serve the Master as a God and as a God the stranger within thy dwelling. The works that are without blame before the people, thou shalt do these with diligence and no others. The deeds we have done that are good and righteous, thou shalt practise these as a religion and no others. Whosoever are better and nobler than we among the Brahmins, thou shalt refresh with a seat to honour them. Thou shalt give with faith and reverence ; without faith thou shalt not give. Thou shalt give with shame, thou shalt give with fear ; thou shalt give with fellow-feeling. Moreover if thou doubt of thy course or of thy action, then to whatsoever Brahmins be there who are careful thinkers, devout, not moved by others, lovers of virtue, not severe or cruel, even as they do in that thing, so do thou. Then as to men accused and arraigned by their fellows, whatsoever Brahmins be there who are careful thinkers, devout, not moved by others, lovers of virtue, not severe or cruel, even as they are towards these, so be thou. This is the law and the teaching. These are the Commandments. In such wise shalt thou practise religion yea, verily, in such wise do ever religiously." (Taittiriya Up. I. 11).

CONSCIOUSNESS—FOURFOLD. The old Indian psychology divided consciousness into three provinces, waking state, dream-state, sleep-state, *jāgrat, svapna, susupti*; and it supposed in the human being a waking self, a dream-self, a sleep-self, with the supreme or absolute self of being, the fourth or Turiya, beyond, of which all these are derivations for the enjoyment of relative experience in the world.

If we examine the phraseology of the old books, we shall find that the waking state is the consciousness of the material universe which we normally possess in this embodied existence dominated by the physical mind. The dream-state is a consciousness corresponding to the subtler life-plane and mind-plane behind, which to us, even when we get intimations of them, have not the same concrete reality as the things of the physical existence. The sleep-state is a consciousness corresponding to the supramental plane proper to the gnosis, which is beyond our experience because our causal body or envelope of gnosis is not developed in us, its faculties not active, and therefore we are in relation to that plane in a condition of dreamless sleep. The Turiya beyond is the consciousness of our pure self-existence or our absolute being with which we have no direct relations at all, whatever mental reflections we may receive in our dream or our waking or even irrecoverably, in our sleep consciousness. This fourfold scale corresponds to the degrees of the ladder of being by which we climb back towards the absolute Divine.

CONSECRATION. Everything in us has constantly to be called back to the central faith and will and vision. Every thought and impulse has to be reminded in the language of the Upanishad that " That is the divine Brahman and not this which men here adore." Every vital fibre has to be persuaded to accept an entire renunciation of all that hitherto represented to it its own existence. Mind has to cease to be mind and become brilliant with something beyond it. Life has to change into a thing vast and calm and intense and powerful that can no longer recognise its old blind eager narrow self or petty impulse and desire. Even the body has to submit to a mutation and be no longer the clamorous animal or the impending clod it now is, but become instead a conscious servant and radiant instrument and living form of the spirit.

CONSISTENCY IN THE UPANISHADS. In real truth the Upanishads are in all their parts, allowing for imaginative language and an occasional element of symbolism, quite rational, consistent and homogeneous. They are not concerned indeed to create an artificial impression of consistency by ignoring the various aspects of this manifold Universe and reducing all things to a single denomination ; for they are not metaphysical treatises aiming at mathematical abstractness or geometrical precision and consistency. They are a great store of observations, and spiritual experiences with conclusions and generalisations from those observations and experiences, set down without any thought of controversial caution or any anxiety to avoid logical contradictions. Yet they have the consistency of all truthful observation and honest experience ; one grand universal truth developed into a certain number of wide general laws within whose general agreement there is room for infinite particular variations and even anomalies. They have in other words a scientific rather than a logical consistency.

COSMIC CONSCIOUSNESS. By entering into the cosmic consciousness we participate in the all-vision and see everything in the values of the Infinite and the One. Limitation itself, ignorance itself change their meaning for us. Ignorance changes into a particular action of divine-knowledge, strength and weakness and incapacity into a free putting forth and holding back various measures of divine Force, joy and grief, pleasure and pain into a mastering and suffering of divine delight, struggle into balancing of forces and values in the divine harmony. We do not suffer by the limitations of our mind, life and body ; for we no longer live in these but in the infinity of the Spirit and these we view in their right value and place and purpose in the manifestation, as degrees of the supreme being, conscious-force and delight of Sachchidananda veiling and manifesting Himself in the cosmos. We cease to judge men and things by their outward appearances and are delivered from hostile and contra-dictory ideas and emotions ; for it is the soul that we see, the Divine that we seek and find in every thing and creature, and the rest has only a secondary value to us in a scheme of relations which exist now for us only as self-expressions of the Divine and not as having any absolute value in themselves. So too no event can disturb us, since the distinction of happy and unhappy, beneficent and maleficent happenings loses its force, and all is seen in its divine value and its divine purpose. Thus we arrive at a perfect liberation and an infinite equality. It is this con-summation of which the Upanishad speaks when it says " He in whom the self has become all existences, how shall he have delusion, whence shall he have grief who knows entirely and sees in all things oneness." * (Isha Up. 7)

COSMIC REALISATION. Besides the consciousness of the transcendent Self pure, self-existent, timeless, spaceless we have to accept and become the cosmic consciousness, we have to identity our being with the Infinite who makes himself the base and continent of the worlds and dwells in all existences. This is the realisation which the ancient Vedantins spoke of as seeing all existences in the self and the self in all existences ; and in addition they speak of the crowning realisation of the man in whom the original miracle of existence has been repeated, self-being has become all these existences that belong to the worlds of the becoming.

COSMIC TREE.   *Vide aśvattha* Tree.

COSMOS.   All world is a movement of the Spirit in itself and is mutable and transcient in all its formations and appearances ;

---

* *vijānataḥ*. Vijnana is the knowledge of the One and the Many, by which the Many are seen in the terms of the One, in the infinite unifying Truth, Right, Vast of the divine existence.

its only eternity is an eternity of recurrence, its only stability a
semblance caused by certain fixities of relation and grouping.

Every separate object in the universe is, in truth, itself the
whole universe presenting a certain front or outward appearance of its movement. The microcosm is one with the macrocosm.

Yet in their relation of principle of movement and result of
movement they are continent and contained, world in world,
jagatyām jagat, movement in movement. The individual therefore partakes of the nature of the universal, refers back to it for
its source of activity, is, as we say, subject to its laws and part
of cosmic Nature.

" One seed arranged by the universal Energy in multitudinous
forms." (Shvetashvatara Up. VI. 12)

CREATION. " The Spirit desired of old ' I would be manifold
for the birth of peoples.' Therefore He concentrated all Himself
in thought, and by the force of His brooding He created all this
universe, yea, all whatsoever exists. Now when He had brought
it forth, He entered into that He had created, He entering in
became the Is here and the May Be there ; He became that which
is defined and that which has no feature ; He became this housed
thing and that houseless ; He became Knowledge and He became
Ignorance ; He became Truth and He became falsehood. Yea,
He became all truth, even whatsoever here exists. Therefore they
say of Him that He is Truth." (Taittiriya Up. II. 6)

" In the beginning all this Universe was Non-Existent and
Unmanifest, from which this manifest Existence was born. Itself
created itself ; none other created it. Therefore they say of it
the well and beautifully made." (Taittiriya Up. II. 7.)

CUPIDITY. " Lust not after any man's possession." (Isha
Up. I).

DAKSINĀYANA. Southern solstice. " The year also is that
Eternal Father and of the year there are two paths, the northern
solstice and the southern. Now they who worship God with the
well dug and the oblation offered, deeming these to be righteousness, conquer their heavens of the Moon : these return again to
the world of birth. Therefore do the souls of sages who have

not yet put from them the desire of offspring, take the way of
the southern solstice which is road of the Fathers. And this also
is Matter, the Female." (Prashna Up. I. 9)

DAWN. As day is a symbol of a time of activity, night a
time of inactivity, so dawn images the imperfect but pregnant
beginnings of regular cosmic action.

Uśas or Dawn, to the early thinker, was the impulse towards
manifest existence, no longer a vague movement in the depths
of the Unmanifest, but already emerging and on the brink of its
satisfaction.

DAY AND NIGHT. Day is the symbol of the continual
manifestation of material things, the *vykta,* the manifest or
fundamentally in *Sat,* in infinite being ; Night is the symbol of
their continual disappearance into *avyakta,* the Unmanifest or
finally into *Asat,* into infinite non-being.

" Day and Night also are the Eternal Father, whereof the Day
is Life and the Night is Matter. Therefore do they offend against
their own life who take joy with woman by day : by night who
take joy, enact holiness." (Prashna Up. I. 13)

DEATH AND AFTER. "Whatsoever be the mind of a man,
with that mind he seeks refuge with the breath when he dies, and
the breath and the upper breath lead him with the Spirit within
him to the world of his imaginings." (Prashna Up. III. 10)

" For some enter a womb to the embodying of the Spirit and
others follow after the Immovable ; according to their deeds is
their goal and after the measure of their revealed knowledge."
(Katha Up. II. 2. 7)

By departing from the physical life one does not disappear
out of the Movement, but only passes into some other general
state of consciousness than the material universe. These states
are either obscure or illuminated, some dark or sunless.

By persisting in gross forms of ignorance, by coercing per-
versely the soul in its self-fulfilment or by a wrong dissolution
of its becoming in the Movement, one enters into states of
blind darkness, not into the worlds of light and of liberated and
blissful being.

Vedantic thought did not envisage rebirth as an immediate entry after death into a new body ; the mental being in man is not so rigidly bound to the vital and physical,—on the contrary, the latter are ordinarily dissolved together after death, and there must therefore be, before the soul is attracted back towards terrestrial existence, an interval in which it assimilates its terrestrial experiences in order to be able to constitute a new vital and physical being upon earth. During this interval it must dwell in states or worlds beyond and these may be favourable (heaven) or unfavourable (hell) to its future development.

Vide Heaven and Hell.

Survival of Personality after Death : In the Katha Upanishad the question is raised in a very instructive fashion, quite apposite to the subject we have in hand. Nachiketas, sent by his father to the world of Death, thus questions Yama, the lord of that world : Of the man who has gone forward, who has passed away from us, some say that he is and others " this he is not " ; which then is right ? What is the truth of the great passage ? Such is the form of the question and at first sight it seems simply to raise the problem of immortality in the European sense of the word, the survival of the identical personality. But that is not what Nachiketas asks. He has already taken as the second of three boons offered to him by Yama the knowledge of the sacred Flame by which man crosses over hunger and thirst, leaves sorrow and fear far behind him and dwells in heaven securely rejoicing. Immortality in that sense he takes for granted as, already standing in that farther world, he must surely do. The knowledge he asks for involves the deeper, finer problem, of which Yama affirms that even the gods debated this of old and it is not easy to know, for subtle is the law of it ; something survives that appears to be the same person, that descends into hell, that ascends into heaven, that returns upon the earth with a new body, but is it really the same person that thus survives ? Can we really say of the man " He still is ", or must we not rather say " This he no longer is " ? Yama too in his answer speaks not at all of the survival of death, and he only gives a verse or two to a bare description of that constant rebirth

which all serious thinkers admitted as a universally acknowledged truth. What he speaks of is the Self, the real Man, the
Lord of all these changing appearances ; without the knowledge
of that Self the survival of the personality is not immortal life
but a constant passing from death to death. He only who
goes beyond personality to the real Person becomes the
Immortal. Till then a man seems indeed to be born again and
again by the force of his knowledge and works, name succeeds
to name, form gives place to form, but there is no immortality.
   Passage of the Knower after Death. " The Spirit who is here
in man and the Spirit who is there in the Sun, lo, it is One
Spirit and there is no other. He who has this knowledge, when
he goes from this world having passed to the Self which is of
food ; having passed to the Self which is of Prana ; having
passed to the Self which is of Mind ; having passed to the Self
which is of Knowledge ; having passed to the Self which is of
Bliss, lo, he ranges about the worlds, he eats what he will, and
takes what shape he will and ever he sings the mighty Sama.
' Ho ! ho ! ho ! I am food ! I am food ! I am food ! I am the
eater of food ! I am the eater ! I am the eater ! I am he who
makes Scripture ! I am he who makes ! I am he who makes !
I am the first born of the Law ; before the gods were, I am, yea,
at the very heart of immortality. He who gives me, verily, he
preserves me ; for I being food, eat him that eats. I have
conquered the whole world and possessed it, my light is as the
sun in its glory '." (Taittiriya Up. III. 10).

DELIVERANCE. " That in which sound is not, nor touch,
nor shape, nor diminution, nor taste, nor smell, that which is
eternal, and It is without end or beginning, higher than the
Great-Self, the stable ; that having seen, from the mouth of
death there is deliverance." (Katha Up. I. 3. 15).

DESIRE. " In the beginning all was covered by Hunger that
is Death ; that made for itself Mind so that it might attain to
possession of self." (Brihadaranyaka Up. I. 2. 1).

DESIRES. " When all the desires that cling to the heart are
loosed away from it, then the mortal becomes immortal, even

here he possesses the Eternal." (Brihadaranyaka Up. IV. 4. 7).

Desires and Spirit : " The wise who are without desire and worship the Spirit pass beyond this sperm. He who cherishes desires and his mind dwells with his longings, is by his desires born again wherever they lead him, but the man who has won all his desires and has found his soul, for him even here, in this world vanish away all desires." (Mundaka Up. III. 2. I-2).

DESTROYER. The Lord of all existence is the universal Creator but also the universal Destroyer, of whom the ancient Scripture can say in a ruthless image, " The sages and the heroes are his food and death is the spice of his banquet." It is one and the same truth seen first indirectly and obscurely in the facts of life and then directly and clearly in the soul's vision of that which manifests itself in life. The outward aspect is that of world-existence and human existence proceeding by struggle and slaughter ; the inward aspect is that of the universal Being fulfilling himself in a vast creation and a vast destruction.

" He to whom the sages are as meat and heroes as food for his eating and Death is an ingredient of His banquet, how thus shall one know of Him where He abides ? " (Katha Up. I.2.25)

DEVA AND ASURA. This distinction is a very ancient one in Indian religious symbolism. The fundamental idea of the Rig Veda is a struggle between the Gods and their dark opponents, between the Masters of Light, sons of Infinity and the children of Division and Night, a battle in which man takes part and which is reflected in all his inner life and action. This was also a fundamental principle of the religion of Zoroaster. The same idea is prominent in later literature. The Ramayana is in its ethical intention the parable of an enormous conflict between the Deva in the human form and the incarnate Rakshasa, between the representative of a high culture and Darma and a huge unbridled force and gigantic civilisation of the exaggerated Ego. The Mahabharata takes for its subject a life-long clash between human Devas and Asuras, the men of power, sons of the Gods, who are governed by the light of a high ethical Dharma and others who are embodied Titans, the men of power who are out for the service of their intellectual, vital and physical ego. The ancient mind, more open than ours, to the truth of things behind the physical veil, saw behind the life of man great cosmic Powers or beings representative of certain turns or grades of the universal Shakti, divine, titanic, gigantic, demoniac, and men who strongly represented in themselves these types of nature were themselves considered as Devas, Asuras, Rakshasas, Pishachas.

DHĪRĀH. The ancient sages who were steadfast in the gaze of their thought, not drawn away from the completeness of knowledge by one light or by another and whose perception of Brahman was consequently entire and comprehensive.

DIVINE BEING. " O fair son, even here is that Being, in the inner body of every creature." (Prashna Up. VI. 2).

" He in whom the members are set as the spokes of a wheel are set in its nave, Him know for the Being Who is the goal of Knowledge, so shall death pass away from you and his anguish." (Prashna Up. VI. 6).

DIVINE LIFE. Enjoyment of the universe and all it contains is the object of world-existence, but renunciation of all in desire is the condition of the free enjoyment of all.

The renunciation demanded is not a moral constraint of self-denial or a physical rejection, but an entire liberation of the spirit from any craving after the forms of things.

The terms of this liberation are freedom from egoism and, consequently, freedom from personal desire. Practically, this renunciation implies that one should not regard anything in the universe as a necessary object of possession, nor as possessed by another and not by oneself, nor as an object of greed in the heart or the senses.

This attitude is founded on the perception of unity. For it has already been said that all souls are one possessing Self, the Lord ; and although the Lord inhabits each object as if separately, yet all objects exist in that Self and not outside it.

Therefore by transcending Ego and realising the one Self, we possess the whole universe in the one cosmic consciousness and do not need to possess physically.

Having by oneness with the Lord the possibility of an infinite free delight in all things, we do not need to desire.

Being one with all beings, we possess, in their enjoyment in ours and in the cosmic Being's, delight of universal self-expression. It is only by this Ananda at once transcendent and universal that man can be free in his soul and yet live in the world with the full active Life of the Lord in His universe of movement.

DIVINE PERSONALITY. The Vedantic idea of God, "He", Deva or Ishvara, must not be confused with the ordinary notions attached to the conception of a Personal God. Personality is generally conceived as identical with individuality and the vulgar idea of a Personal God is a magnified individual like man in His nature but yet different, greater, more vast and all overpowering. Vedanta admits the human manifestation of Brahman in man and to man, but does not admit that this is the real nature of the Ishvara.

God is Sachchidananda. He manifests Himself as infinite existence of which the essentiality is consciousness, of which again the essentiality is the bliss, is self-delight. Delight cognising variety of itself, seeking its own variety, as it were, becomes the universe. But these are abstract terms ; abstract ideas in themselves cannot produce concrete realities. They are impersonal states ; impersonal states cannot in themselves produce personal activities.

This becomes still clearer if we consider the manifestation of Sachchidananda. In that manifestation Delight translates itself into Love ; Consciousness translates itself into double terms, conceptive Knowledge, executive Force ; Existence translates into Being, that is to say, into Person and Substance. But Love is incomplete without a Lover and an object of Love, Knowledge without a Knower and an object of Knowledge, Force without a Worker and a Work, Substance without a Person cognising and constituting it.

This is because the original terms also are not really impersonal abstractions. In delight of Brahman there is an Enjoyer of delight, in consciousness of Brahman a Conscient, in existence of Brahman an Existent ; but the object of Brahman's delight and consciousness and the term and stuff of Its existence are Itself. In the divine Being Knowledge, the Knower and the Known and, therefore, necessarily also Delight, the Enjoyer and the Enjoyed are one.

The Self-Awareness and Self-Delight of Brahman has two modes of its Force of consciousness, its Prakriti or Maya, — intensive in self-absorption, diffusive in self-extension. The intensive mode is proper to the pure and silent Brahman ; the diffusive to the active Brahman. It is the diffusion of the Self-existent in the term and stuff of His own existence that we call the world, the becoming or the perpetual movement (*bhuvanam, jagat*). It is Brahman that becomes ; what He becomes is also the Brahman. The object of Love is the self of the Lover ; the work is the self-figuration of the Worker ; Universe is body and action of the Lord.

When, therefore, we consider the abstract and impersonal aspect of the infinite existence, we say, " That ", when we consider the Existent self-aware and self-blissful, we say, " He ". Neither conception is entirely complete. Brahman itself is the Unknowable beyond all conceptions of Personality and Impersonality. We may call it " That " to show that we exile from our affirmation all term and definition. We may equally call it " He ", provided we speak with the same intention of rigorous exclusion. *Tat* and *sah* are always the same. One that escapes definition.

In the universe there is a constant relation of Oneness and Multiplicity. This expresses itself as the universal Personality and the many persons, and both between the One and the Many and among the Many themselves there is the possibility of an infinite variety of relations. These relations are determined by the play of the divine existence, the Lord, entering into His manifested habitations. They exist at first as conscious relations between individual souls ; they are then taken up by them and used as a means of entering into conscious relation with the One. It is this entering into various relation with the One which is the object and function of Religion. All religions are justified by this essential necessity ; all express one Truth in various ways and move by various paths to one goal.

The Divine Personality reveals Himself in various forms and names to the individual soul. These forms and names are in a sense created in the human consciousness ; in another they are eternal symbols revealed by the Divine who thus concretises Himself in mind-form to the multiple consciousness and aids it in its return to its own Unity. (It would be an error to suppose that conceptions are in their essence later developments of philosophical Hinduism. The conception of the many forms and names of the One is as old as the Rig Veda).

DIVINE PURUSHA. In all things there is a presence, a primal Reality, — the Self, the Divine, Brahman, — which is for ever pure, perfect, blissful, infinite ; its infinity is not affected by the limitations of relative things ; its purity is not stained by our sin and evil ; its bliss is not touched by our pain and suffering ; its perfection is not impaired by our defects of consciousness, knowledge, will, unity. In certain images of the Upanishads the divine Purusha is described as the one Fire which has entered into all forms and shapes itself according to the form, as the one Sun which illumines all impartially and is not affected by the faults of our seeing.

DREAM STATE AND DREAMLESS SLEEP. Yajnavalkya in the Brihadaranyaka Upanishad states very positively that there are two planes or states of the being which are two worlds, and that in the dream state one can see both worlds, for the dream state is intermediate between them, it is their joining-plane. It is clear he is speaking of a subliminal condition of the consciouness which can carry in it communications between the physical and the supraphysical worlds.

The description of the dreamless sleep applies both to deep sleep and to the condition of trance in which one enters into a massed consciousness containing in it all the powers of being but all compressed within itself and concentrated solely on itself, and, when active, then active in a consciousness where all is the self ; this is, clearly, a state admitting us into the higher planes of the spirit normally now superconscient to our waking being.

DOORS OUTWARD. "The self-born has set the doors of sense to face outwards, therefore the soul of a man gazes outward and not at the Self within : hardly a wise man here and there desiring immortality, turns his eyes inward and sees the Self within him." (Katha Up. II. 1. 1)

DUAL STATUS OF THE SOUL. There is one unborn of three colours, says a text, the eternal feminine principle of Prakriti with its three gunas, ever creating ; there are two unborn, two Purushas, of whom one cleaves to and enjoys her, the other abandons her because he has enjoyed all her enjoyments. In another verse they are described as two birds on one tree, eternally yoked companions, one of whom eats the fruits of the tree, — the Purusha in Nature enjoying her cosmos, — the other eats not, but watches his fellow, the silent Witness, withdrawn from the enjoyment ; when the first sees the second and knows that all is his greatness, then he is delivered from sorrow. The point of view in the two verses is different, but they have a common implication. One of the birds is the eternally silent, unbound Self or Purusha by whom all this is extended and he regards the cosmos he has extended, but is aloof from it ; the other is the Purusha involved in Prakriti. The first verse indicates that the two are the same, represent different states, bound and liberated, of the same conscious being, — for the second unborn has descended into enjoyment of Nature and withdrawn from her ; the other verse brings out what we would not gather from the former, that in its higher status of unity the self is for ever free, inactive unattached, though it descends in its lower being into the multiplicity of the creatures of Prakriti and withdraws from it by reversion in any individual creature to the higher status.

"Two unborn, the Knower and one who knows not, the Lord and one who has not mastery ; one Unborn and in her are the object of enjoyment and the enjoyer." (Shvetashvatara Up. I. 9)

"The soul seated on the same tree of Nature is absorbed and deluded and has sorrow because it is not the Lord, but when it sees and is in union with that other self and greatness of it which is the Lord, then sorrow passes away from it." (Shvetashvatara Up. IV. 7)

DUALITY. " He who has the knowledge ' I am Brahman ' becomes all this that is ; but whoever worships another divinity than the one Self and thinks, ' Other is he and I am other,' he knows not." (Brihadaranyaka Up. I. 4. 10)

DUALITIES. Pleasure and pain are the vital or sensational deformations given by the lower energy to the spontaneous Ananda or delight of the spirit when brought into contact with her workings. Liking and disliking are the corresponding mental deformations given by her to the reactive Will of the spirit that determines its response to her contacts. These dualities are the positive and negative terms in which the ego-soul of the lower nature enjoys the universe. The negative terms, pain, dislike, sorrow, repulsion and the rest, are perverse or at the best ignorantly reverse responses ; the positive terms, liking, pleasure, joy, attraction, are ill-guided responses or at the best insufficient and in character inferior to those of the true spiritual experience.

DVA SUPARNĀ. Two birds, beautiful of wing, close companions, cling to one common tree : of the two one eats the sweet fruit of the tree, the other eats not but watches his fellow. The soul is the bird that sits immersed on the one common tree ; but because he is not the lord he is bewildered and has sorrow. But when he sees that other who is the Lord and beloved, he knows that all is His greatness and his sorrow passes away from him. When, a seer, he sees the Golden-hued, the maker, the Lord, the Spirit who is the source of Brahman, then he becomes the knower and shakes from his wings sin and virtue ; pure of all stain he reaches the supreme identity. (Mundaka Up. III. 1-3)
Vide Dual status of the soul.

DWARF. " This is he that draws the main breath upward and casts the lower breath downward. The Dwarf that sits in the centre, to Him all the Gods do homage." (Katha Up. II. 2. 3)

EARTH. Earth is the footing, *pājasyam,* because matter, outward form, is the fundamental condition for the manifesta-

tion of life, mind and all higher forces. On Matter we rest and
have our firm stand ; out of Matter we rise to our fulfilment in
Spirit.

EARTHY. " He that thinks this world is and there is no
other, comes again and again into Death's thraldom." (Katha
Up. I. 2. 6)

EGO. Ego is only a faculty put forward by the discrimina-
tive mind to centralise round itself the experiences of the sense-
mind and to serve as a sort of lynch-pin in the wheel which keeps
together the movement. It is no more than an instrument,
although it is true that so long as we are limited by our normal
mentality, we are compelled by the nature of that mentality and
the purpose of the instrument to mistake our ego-function for
our very self.

EPOCH OF THE UPANISHADS. The Upanishads have
always been recognised in India as the crown and end of the
Veda ; that is indicated in their general name, Vedanta. And
they are in fact a large crowning outcome of the Vedic discipline
and experience. The time in which the Vedantic truth was
wholly seen and the Upanishads took shape, was, as we can
discern from such records as the Chhandogya and Brihadaranyaka, an epoch of immense and strenuous seeking, an intense and
ardent seed-time of the Spirit. In the stress of that seeking the
truths held by the initiates but kept back from ordinary men
broke their barriers, swept through the higher mind of the
nation and fertilised the soil of Indian culture for a constant
and ever increasing growth of spiritual consciousness and
spiritual experience. This turn was not as yet universal ; it
was chiefly men of the higher classes, Kshatriyas and Brahmins
trained in the Vedic system of education, no longer content with
an external truth and the works of the outer sacrifice, who
began everywhere to seek the highest word of revealing experience from the sages who possessed the knowledge of the One.
But we find too among those who attained to the knowledge and
became great teachers men of inferior or doubtful birth like
Janashruti, the wealthy Shudra, or Satyakama Jabali, son of a

servant-girl who knew not who was his father. The work that was done in this period became the firm bedrock of Indian spirituality in later ages and from it gush still the life-giving waters of a perennial never-failing inspiration. This period, this activity, this grand achievement created the whole difference between the evolution of Indian civilisation and the quite different curve of other cultures.

ETHICS. All ethics is a construction of good in a Nature which has been smitten with evil by the powers of darkness born of the Ignorance, even as it is expressed in the ancient legend of the Vedanta.

To rise beyond virtue and sin, good and evil is an essential part of the Vedantic idea of liberation. For liberation signifies an emergence into the true spiritual nature of being where all action is the automatic self-expression of that truth and there can be nothing else.

EVIL. *Vide* Falsehood.

EVOLUTION. Priority of the animal over man in the time succession : a Upanishad declares that the Self or Spirit after deciding on life creation first formed animal kind like the cow or horse, but the gods, — who are in the thought of the Upanishads powers of Consciousness and powers of Nature, — found them to be insufficient vehicles, and the Spirit finally created the form of man which the gods saw to be excellently made and sufficient and they entered into it for their cosmic functions. This is a clear parable of the creation of more and more developed forms till one was found that was capable of housing a developed consciousness.

"From the non-being to the true being, from the darkness to the Light, from death to Immortality." (Brihadaranyaka Up. I. 3. 28)

EXISTENCE. "One indivisible that is pure existence." (Chhandogya Up. VI. 2. 1)

Three Aspects of Existence : The first is based upon that self-knowledge which, in our human realisation of the Divine, the

Upanishad describes as the Self in us becoming all existences ;
the second on that which is described as seeing all existences in
the Self ; the third on that which is described as seeing the Self
in all existences. The Self becoming all existences is the basis
of our oneness with all ; the Self containing all existences is the
basis of our oneness in difference ; the Self inhabiting all is the
basis of our individuality in the universal.

> *Three States of Existence* :   The human and mortal, the
Brahman-consciousness which is the absolute of our relativities,
and the utter absolute which is unknowable. The first is in a
sense a false status of misrepresentation because it is a continual
term of apparent opposites and balancing where the truth of
things is a secret unity ; we have here a bright or positive figure
and a dark or negative figure and both are figures, neither the
Truth ; still in what we now live and through that we have to
move to the Beyond. The second is the Lord of all this dual
action who is beyond it ; He is the truth of Brahman and not
in any way a falsehood or misrepresentation, but the truth of
it as attained by us in our eternal supramental being ; in Him
are the absolutes of all that here we experience in partial figures.
The Unknowable is beyond our grasp because though it
is the same Reality, yet it exceeds even our highest terms
of eternal being and is beyond Existence and Non-Existence ;
it is therefore to the Brahman, the Lord who has a relation to what we are that we must direct our search if
we would attain beyond what temporarily seem to what
eternally is.

FAILURE. " Yea, he that is without knowledge and is un-
mindful and is ever unclean reaches not that goal, but wanders
in the cycle of phenomena." (Katha Up. 1. 3, 7)

FAITH. " Not with the mind has man the power to get God,
no, nor through speech, nor by the eye. Unless one says ' He
is ' how can one become sensible of Him ?

One must apprehend God in the concept ' He Is ' and also in
His essential : but when he has grasped Him as the ' Is ', then
the essential of God dawns upon a man." (Katha Up. II. 3.
12-13)

FALL. The sense of ego is a fall from truth of our being. (Mahopanishad. V. 2)

FALSEHOOD. " The first and the highest are truth ; in the middle there is falsehood, but it is taken between the truth on both sides of it and it draws its being from the truth." (Brihad-aranyaka Up. V. 5. 1)

The truth of the physical reality and the truth of the spiritual and superconscient reality. Into the intermediate subjective and mental realities which stand between them, falsehood can enter, but takes either truth from above or truth from below as the substance out of which it builds itself and both are pressing upon it to turn its misconstructions into truth of life and truth of spirit.

" They live according to another idea of self than the reality, deluded, attached, expressing a falsehood, — as if by an enchantment they see the false as the true." (Maitri Up. VII. 10)

" They live and move in Ignorance and go round and round, battered and stumbling, like blind men led by one who is blind." (Mundaka Up. I. 2. 8)

Falsehood and Evil are very clearly results of the Ignorance and cannot exist where there is no Ignorance ; they can have no self-existence in the Divine Being, they cannot be native elements of the Supreme Nature. If Ignorance disappears into Knowledge, evil and falsehood can no longer endure ; for both are fruits of unconsciousness and wrong consciousness and, if true or whole consciousness is there replacing Ignorance, they have no longer any basis for their existence. These things are a by-product of the world-movement : the sombre flowers of falsehood and suffering and evil have their root in the black soil of the Inconscient.

" I cannot tell thee a lie : for from the roots he shall wither who speaks falsehood." (Prashna Up. VI. 1)

FEAR. " When the Spirit that is within us finds the Invisible, Bodiless, Undefinable and Unhoused Eternal his refuge and firm foundation, then he has passed beyond the reach of Fear. But when the Spirit that is within us makes for himself even a little difference in the Eternal, then he has fear, yea, the Eternal

himself becomes a terror to such a knower who thinks not."
(Taittiriya Up. II. 7)

Fear of the Eternal : " Through the fear of Him the Wind
blows ; through the fear of Him the Sun rises ; through the fear
of Him Indra and Agni and Death hasten in their courses."
(Taittiriya Up. II. 8)

FIVE SHEATHS.   This body, as ancient occult science
discovered, is not the whole even of our physical being ; this
gross density is not all of our substance.   The oldest Vedantic
knowledge tells us of five degrees of our being, the material,
the vital, the mental, the ideal, the spiritual or beatific and to
each of these grades of our soul there corresponds a grade of
our substance, a sheath as it was called in the ancient figurative language.   A later psychology found that these five
sheaths of our substance were the material of three bodies,
gross physical, subtle and causal, in all of which the soul
actually and simultaneously dwells, although here and now
we are superficially conscious only of the material vehicle.
But it is possible to become conscious in our other bodies
as well.

FLAME, SOURCE OF THE WORLD.   The Divine Force
concealed in the subconscient, is that which has originated and
built up the worlds.   At the other end in the superconscient it reveals itself as the Divine Being, Lord and Knower
who has manifested Himself out of the Brahman. (Katha Up.
I. 1. 15)

FORM.   The indwelling secret consciousness inherent and
intrinsic in the Energy that constitutes the object effectualises
and maintains the form by the silent occult Idea in it.   It
differentiates itself according to the form of Matter in a corresponding form of self-being, *rūpam rūpam pratirūpo babhūva*.
(Katha Up. II. 2. 9)

FORTNIGHTS—BRIGHT AND DARK.   " The month also
is that Eternal Father, whereof the dark fortnight is Matter, the
Female and the bright fortnight is Life, the Male.   Therefore do

one manner of sages offer sacrifice in the bright fortnight and another in the dark." (Prashna Up. I. 12)

GANDHRVAS. Gandharvas, Yakshas, Kinnaras are a particular class of beings whose unifying characteristic is material ease, prosperity and a beautiful, happy and undisturbed self indulgence ; they are angels of joy, ease, art, beauty and pleasure.

Their *vāhana* (vehicle) is the *vājin,* the Horse full of ease and plenty, the support of these qualities.

GLOOM. " Sunless are those worlds and enveloped in blind gloom whereto all they in their passing hence resort who are slayers of their souls." (Isha Up. 3)

Vide Death and after.

GOD. " God has not set his body within the ken of seeing, neither does any man with the eye behold Him, but to the heart and the mind and the super-mind He is manifest." (Katha Up. II. 3. 9)

GOD AND NATURE. Phenomenal Nature is a movement of the conscious Lord. The object of the movement is to create forms of His consciousness in motion in which He as the one soul in many bodies can take up his habitation and enjoy the multiplicity and the movement with all their relations.

GODHEAD AND EVOLUTION. " The one Godhead secret in all beings, all-pervading, the inner Self of all, presiding over all action, witness, conscious knower and absolute. The One in control over the many who are passive to Nature, fashions one seed in many ways." (Shvetashvatara Up. VI. 11. 12)

" The Godhead moves in this Field modifying each web of things separately in many ways. One, he presides over all wombs and natures ; himself the womb of all, he is that which brings the ripeness to the nature of the being and he gives to all who have to be matured their result of development and appoints

4

all qualities to their workings." (Ibid. V. 3-5)

"He fashions one form of things in many ways." (Katha Up. II. 2. 12)

GOD-REALISATION. The ordinary man who wishes to reach God through knowledge, must undergo an elaborate training. He must begin by becoming absolutely pure, he must cleanse thoroughly his body, his heart and his intellect, he must get himself a new heart and be born again ; for only the twice-born can understand or teach the Vedas. When he has done this he needs yet four things before he can succeed, the *śruti* or recorded revelation, the Sacred Teacher, the practice of Yoga and the Grace of God.

The business of *śruti* and especially of the Upanishads is to seize the mind and draw it into a magic circle, to accustom it to the thoughts and aspirations of God (after the Supreme), to bathe it in certain ideas, surround it with a certain spiritual atmosphere ; for this purpose it plunges and rolls the mind over and over in an ocean of marvellous sound through which a certain train of associations goes ever rolling. In other words it appeals through the intellect, the ear and the imagination to the soul. But even when he has steeped himself in the Upanishad, he may have understood what the Upanishad suggests, but he has not understood all that it implies, the great mass of religious truth that lies behind, of which the Upanishad is but a hint or an echo. For this he must go to the Teacher. "Awake, ye, arise and learn of God, seeking out the Best who have the Knowledge." Hard is it in these days to find the Best, for the Best do not come to us, we have to show our sincerity, patience and perseverance by seeking them. And when we have heard the whole of the *Brahmavidyā* from the Teacher, we still know of God by theory only ; we must further learn from a preceptor the practical knowledge of God, the vision of Him and attainment of Him which is Yoga and the goal of Yoga. And even in that we cannot succeed unless we have the Grace of God ; for Yoga is beset with temptations not the least of which are the powers it gives us, which the ignorant call super-natural. Only the Grace of God can keep us firm and help us over the temptations. Truly does the Upanishad say, "Sharp as a razor's edge is the path difficult and hard to traverse, say the seers."

GODS. The Gods of the Upanishads have been supposed to be a figure for the senses, but although they act in the senses, they are yet much more than that. They represent the divine power in its great and fundamental cosmic functionings whether in man or in mind and life and Matter in general ; they are not the functionings themselves but something of the Divine which is essential to their operation and its immediate possessor and cause. They are positive self-representations of the Brahman leading to good, joy, light, love, immortality as against all that is a dark negation of these things. And it is necessarily in the mind, life, senses and speech of man that the battle reaches its height and approaches to its full meaning. The gods seek to lead these to good and light ; the Titans, sons of darkness, seek to pierce them with ignorance and evil. Behind the gods is the Master-Consciousness of which they are the positive cosmic self-representations.

The gods of the Upanishad differ in one all-important respect from the gods of the Rig Veda ; for the latter are not only powers of the One, but conscious of their source and true identity ; they know the Brahman, they dwell in the supreme Godhead, their origin, home and proper plane is the superconscient Truth. It is true they manifest themselves in man in the form of human faculties and assume the appearance of human limitations, manifest themselves in the lower cosmos and assume the mould of its cosmic operations ; but this is only their lesser and lower movement and beyond it they are for ever the One, the Transcendent and Wonderful, the Master of Force and Delight and Knowledge and Being. But in the Upanishads the Brahman idea has grown and cast down the gods from this high pre-eminence so that they appear only in their lesser human and cosmic workings. Much of their other Vedic aspects they keep.

The Aryan gods were *devas*, angels of joy and brightness, fulfilled in being, in harmony with their functions and surroundings, not like the Titans imperfect, dispossessed, struggling.

52 Golden Lid

Their *vāhana* (vehicle) is the *haya*. Firmly seated on the bounding joy of the Horse (*haya*) they deliver themselves confidently to the exultation of his movements.

Gods and Unrevelation : " The gods love the veil of Unrevelation, yea, verily, the gods love the unrevelation." (Aitareya Up. I. 3. 14)

GOLDEN LID. " The face of Truth is covered with a brilliant golden lid ; that do thou remove, O Fosterer, for the law of the Truth, for sight." (Isha Up. 15)

GRACE. " The Self is not to be won by eloquent teaching, nor by brain power, nor by much learning : but only he whom this Being chooses can win Him ; for to him this Self bears His body." (Katha Up. I. 2. 23)

" This Self is not won by exegesis, nor by brain-power, nor by much learning of Scripture. Only by him whom It chooses can it be won ; to him this Self unveils its own body." (Mundaka Up. III. 2. 3)

GRIEF. All grief is born of the shrinking of the ego from the contacts of existence, its sense of fear, weakness, want, dislike, etc. ; and this is born from the delusion of separate existence, the sense of being my separate ego exposed to all these contacts of so much that is not myself.

" He in whom it is the Self-Being that has become all existences that are Becomings, for he has the perfect knowledge, how shall he be deluded, whence shall he have grief who sees everywhere oneness." (Isha Up. 7)

GROWTH INTO THE DIVINE. Whatever we see of the Divine and fix our concentrated effort upon it, that we can become or grow into some kind of unity with it or at the lowest into tune and harmony with it. The old Upanishad put it trenchantly in its highest terms, " Whoever envisages it as the existence becomes that existence and whoever envisages it as the non-existence, becomes that non-existence." So too it is with all else that we see of the Divine, — that, we may say, is at once the essential and pragmatic truth of the Godhead.

GUHĀHITA. "Vast is That, divine, its form unthinkable ; it shines out subtler than the subtle : very far and farther than farness, it is here close to us, for those who have vision it is even here in this world ; it is here, hidden in the secret heart." (Mundaka Up. III. 1. 7)

"Finer than the fine, huger than the huge, the self hides in the secret heart of the creature : when a man strips himself of will and is weaned from sorrow then he beholds Him." (Katha Up. I. 2. 20)

"He is established in our secret being and lodged in the cavern heart of things." (Katha Up. I. 2. 12)

GURU. "An inferior man cannot tell you of Him ; for thus told thou canst not truly know Him, since He is thought of in many aspects. Yet unless told of Him by another thou canst not find thy way to Him ; for He is subtler than subtlety and that which logic cannot reach.

This wisdom is not to be had by reasoning ; only when told thee by another it brings a real knowledge." (Katha Up. I. 2. 8, 9)

"Let whosoever seeks for success and well-being approach with homage a self-knower." (Mundaka Up. III. 1. 10)

"Arise, awake, find out the great ones and learn of them : for sharp as a razor's edge, hard to traverse, difficult of going is that path, say the sages." (Katha Up. I. 3. 14)

"The seeker of the Brahman, having put to the test the worlds piled up by works, arrives at world-distaste, for not by work done is reached He who is Uncreated. For the knowledge of That, let him approach, fuel in hand, a Guru one who is learned in the Veda and is devoted to contemplation of the Brahman. To him because he has taken entire refuge with him, with a heart tranquillised and a spirit at peace, that man of knowledge declares in its principles the science of the Brahman by which one comes to know the Immutable Spirit, the True and Real." (Mundaka Up. I. 2. 12-13)

"Thou art our father who has carried us over to the other side of the Ignorance." (Prashna Up. VI. 8)

HAYA. Bearer of the gods, of a swift, free, joyous, bounding motion.
Vide Gods.

HE AM I. "The Lustre which is thy most blessed form of all, that in Thee I behold. The Purusha there and there, He am I." (Isha Up. 16)

HEART. The heart in Vedic psychology is not restricted to the seat of the emotions ; it includes all that large tract of spontaneous mentality, nearest to the subconscient in us, out of which rise the sensations, emotions, instincts, impulses and all those intuitions and inspirations that travel through these agencies before they arrive at form in the intelligence. This is the "heart" of Veda and Vedanta, *hṛdaya, hṛd* or *brahman.* There in the present state of mankind the Purusha is supposed to be seated centrally.

The heart spoken of by the Upanishads corresponds with the physical cardiac centre ; it is the *hṛtpadma* of the Tantriks. As a subtle centre, *cakra*, it is supposed to have its apex on the spine and to broaden out in front.

HEART-ETHER. "Lo, this heaven of ether which is in the heart within, there dwells the Being who is all Mind, the radiant and golden Immortal." (Taittiriya Up. I. 6)

HEAVEN AND HELL. The Vedantic heavens are states of light and the soul's expansion ; darkness, self-obscuration and self-distortion are the nature of the Hells which it has to shun.

HEAVENLY FLAME. The celestial force concealed subconsciently in man's mortality by the kindling of which and its right ordering man transcends his earthly nature ; not the physical flame of the external sacrifice. (Katha Up. I. 1. 13)

HEREDITY. I enter into birth, not in a separate being, but in the life of the whole, and therefore I inherit the life of the whole. I am born physically by a generation which is a carrying on of its unbroken history ; the body, life, physical mentality of all past being prolongs itself in me and I must therefore undergo the law of heredity ; the parent, says the Upanishad, recreates himself by the energy in his seed and is reborn in the child.

HIGHEST GOAL. " Than the senses the objects of sense are higher : and higher than the objects of sense is the Mind : and higher than the Mind is the faculty of knowledge : and than that the Great-Self is higher. And higher than the Great-Self is the Unmanifest and higher than the Unmanifest is the Purusha : than the Purusha there is none higher : He is the culmination, He is the highest goal of the journey." (Katha Up. I. 3. 10, 11)

HIRANMAYA PURUSHA. Vide Self of Knowledge.

HIRANYA-GARBHA. Brahman manifest in the Universe of subtle Matter (penetrating and surrounding the gross) as the Creator, Self and Container, styled the Golden Embryo of life and form.

HṚDAYA GRANTHI. Heart-strings. " When every desire that finds lodging in the heart of man, has been loosened from its moorings, then this mortal puts on immortality : even here he tastes God, in this human body.
Yea, when all the strings of the heart are rent asunder, even here, in this human birth, then the mortal becomes immortal. This is the whole teaching of the Scriptures." (Katha Up. II. 3. 14-15)
" The knot of the heart-strings is rent, cut away are all doubts, and a man's works are spent and perish, when is seen That which is at once the being below and the Supreme. In a supreme golden sheath the Brahman lies, stainless, without parts. A splendour is That, It is the Light of Lights, It is That which the self-knowers know." (Mundaka Up. II. 2. 9-10)
" He, verily, who knows that Supreme Brahman becomes himself Brahman ; in his lineage none is born who knows not the Brahman. He crosses beyond sorrow, he crosses beyond

sin, he is delivered from the knotted cord of the secret heart
and becomes immortal." (Mundaka Up. III. 2. 9)

HUMAN CHARIOT.   "Know the body for a chariot and
the soul for the master of the chariot ; know Reason for the
charioteer and the mind for the reins only.

The senses they speak as the steeds and the objects of sense
as the paths in which they move ; and One yoked with self and
the mind and the senses, as the enjoyer, say the thinkers."
(Katha Up. I. 3. 3, 4)

HUNDRED YEARS.   "Doing verily works in this world one
should wish to live a hundred years." (Isha Up. 2)

HUNGER.   Hunger that is Death, said the old Upanishads,
is the creator and master of this world, and they figured vital
existence in the image of the Horse of the sacrifice.   Matter
they described by a name which means ordinarily food and they
said, we call it food because it is devoured and devours
creatures.   The eater eating is eaten, this is the formula of the
material world, as the Darwinians rediscovered when they laid
it down that the struggle for life is the law of evolutionary
existence.

Life, says the Upanishad, is Hunger which is Death, and by
this Hunger which is Death, *aśanāyā mṛtyuḥ*, the material world
has been created.   For Life here assumes as its mould material
substance, and material substance is Being infinitely divided
and seeking infinitely to aggregate itself ; between these two
impulses of infinite division and infinite aggregation the
material existence of the universe is constituted.   The attempt
of the individual, the living atom, to maintain and aggrandise
itself is the whole sense of Desire ; a physical, vital, moral,
mental increase by a more and more all-embracing experience,
a more and more all-embracing possession, absorption,
assimilation, enjoyment is the inevitable, fundamental, ineradi-
cable impulse of Existence, once divided and individualised,
yet ever secretly conscious of its all-embracing, all-possessing
infinity.   The impulse to realise that secret consciousness is the
spur of the cosmic Divine, the lust of the embodied Self within

every individual creature ; and it is inevitable, just, salutary that it should seek to realise it first in the terms of life by an increasing growth and expansion. In the physical world this can only be done by feeding on the environment, by aggrandising oneself through the absorption of others or of what is possessed by others ; and this necessity is the universal justification of Hunger in all its forms. Still what devours must also be devoured, for the law of interchange, of action and reaction, of limited capacity and therefore of a final exhaustion and succumbing governs all life in the physical world.

IGNORANCE. " They live and move in the Ignorance and go round and round, battered and stumbling, like blind men led by one who is blind." (Mundaka Up. I. 2. 8)

IHAIVA. The Divine that we adore is not only a remote extra-cosmic Reality, but a half-veiled Manifestation present and near to us here in the universe. Life is the field of a divine manifestation not yet complete : here, in life, on earth, in the body, — *ihaiva*, as the Upanishads insist, — we have to unveil the Godhead ; here we must make its transcendent greatness, light and sweetness real to our consciousness, here possess and, as far as may be, express it.

It is here, *ihaiva,* in this mortal life and body that immortality must be won, here in this lower Brahman and by this embodied soul that the Higher must be known and possessed. " If here one find it not, great is the perdition." This life-force in us is led forward by the attraction of the supreme Life on its path of constant acquisition through types of the Brahman until it reaches a point where it has to go entirely forward, to go across out of the mortal life, the mortal vision of things to some Beyond. So long as death is not entirely conquered, this going beyond is represented in the terms of death and by a passing into other worlds where death is not present, where a type of immortality is tasted corresponding to that which we have found here in our soul-experience ; but the attraction of death and limitation is not overpassed because they still conceal something of immortality and infinity which we have not yet achieved ; therefore there is a necessity of return, an

insistent utility of farther life in the mortal body which we do
not overcome until we have passed beyond all types to the
very being of the Infinite, One and Immortal.

" If *here* one comes to that knowledge, then one truly is ; if
here one comes not to the knowledge, then great is the
perdition." (Kena Up. II. 5)

" If in this world of men and before thy body fall from
thee, thou wert able to apprehend it, then thou availeth for
embodiment in the worlds that He creates." (Katha Up.
II. 3. 4)

ILLUSIONIST IDEA. It is constantly affirmed in the
Upanishads that all this that is is the Brahman, the Reality.
The Brahman becomes all these beings ; all beings must be seen
in the Self, the Reality, and the Reality must be seen in them,
the Reality must be seen as being actually all these beings ; for
not only the Self is Brahman, but all is the Self, all this that is
is the Brahman, the Reality. That emphatic asseveration leaves
no room for an illusory Maya ; but still the insistent denial that
there is anything other than or separate from the experiencing
self, certain phrases used and the description of two of the
states of consciousness as sleep and dream may be taken as if
they annulled the emphasis on the universal Reality ; these
passages open the gates to the illusionist idea and have been
made the foundation for an uncompromising system of that
nature.

IMAGERY OF THE UPANISHADS. The imagery of the
Upanishads is in large part developed from the type of imagery
of the Veda and though very ordinarily it prefers an unveiled
clarity of directly illuminative image, not unoften also it uses
the same symbols in a way that is closely akin to the spirit and
to the less technical part of the method of the older symbolism.
It is to a great extent this element no longer seizable by our
way of thinking that has baffled certain western scholars and
made them cry out that these scriptures are a mixture of the
sublimest philosophical speculations with the first awkward
stammerings of the child mind of humanity. The Upanishads
are not a revolutionary departure from the Vedic mind and its

temperament and fundamental ideas, but a continuation and development and to a certain extent an enlarging transformation in the sense of bringing out into open expression all that was held covered in the symbolic Vedic speech as a mystery and a secret. It begins by taking up the imagery and the ritual symbols of the Veda and the Brahmanas and turning them in such a way as to bring out an inner and mystic sense which will serve as a sort of psychical starting-point for its own more highly evolved and more purely spiritual philosophy. There are a number of passages especially in the prose Upanishads which are entirely of this kind and deal, in a manner recondite, obscure and even unintelligible to the modern understanding, with the psychic sense of ideas then current in the Vedic religious mind, the distinction between the three kinds of Veda, the three worlds and other similar subjects ; but, leading as they do in the thought of the Upanishads to deepest spiritual truths, these passages cannot be dismissed as childish aberrations of the intelligence void of sense or of any discoverable bearing on the higher thought in which they culminate. On the contrary we find that they have a deep significance once we can get inside their symbolic meaning. That appears in a psycho-physical passing upward into a psycho-spiritual knowledge for which we would now use more intellectual, less concrete and imaged terms, but which is still valid for those who practise Yoga and rediscover the secrets of our psycho-physical and psycho-spiritual being. Typical passages of this kind of peculiar expression of psychic truths are Ajatashatru's explanation of sleep and dream or the passages of the Prashna Upanishad on the vital principle and its motions, or those in which the Vedic idea of the struggle between the Gods and the demons is taken up and given its spiritual significance and the Vedic godheads more openly than in Rik and Saman characterised and invoked in their inner function and spiritual power.

IMMANENT DIVINE. The Lord is not only in the Self, but in Nature. He is in the heart of every creature and guides by his presence the turnings of this great natural mechanism. He is present in all, all lives in him, all is himself because all is a becoming of his being, a portion or a figure of his existence.

According to the ancient teaching the seat of the immanent Divine, the hidden Purusha, is in the mystic heart. — the secret heart-cave, *hṛdaye guhāyām*, as the Upanishads put it, — and, according to the experience of many Yogins, it is from its depths that there comes the voice or the breath of the inner oracle.

IMMORTALITY. Does not mean the survival of the self or the ego after dissolution of the body. By immortality is meant the consciousness which is beyond birth and death, beyond the chain of cause and effect, beyond all bondage and limitation, free, blissful, self-existent in conscious-being, the consciousness of the Lord, of the supreme Purusha, of Sachchidananda.

Enjoyment of Immortality : The enjoyment of the infinite delight of existence free from ego, founded on oneness of all in the Lord.

IMMUTABLE. The Immutable is the still and secret foundation of the play and the movement, extended equally, impartially in all things, lending its support to all without choice or active participation. Secure and free in his eternal immutability the Lord projects Himself into the play and the movement, becoming there in His self-existence all that the Seer in Him visualises and the Thinker in Him conceives.

INCONSISTENCY IN THE UPANISHADS. To the rigorous logician bound in his narrow prison of verbal reasoning, the Upanishads seem indeed to base themselves on an initial and fundamental inconsistency. There are a number of passages in these Scriptures which dwell with striking emphasis on the unknowableness of the Absolute Brahman. It is distinctly stated that neither mind nor sense can reach the Brahman and that words return baffled from the attempt to describe It ; more, — that we do not discern the Absolute and Transcendent in Its reality, nor can we discriminate the right way or perhaps any way of teaching the reality of It to others ; and it is even held, that It can only be properly characterised in negative language and that to every challenge for definition the only true answer is *Neti Neti*, It is not this, It is not that. Brahman is not definable, not describable, not intellectually knowable. And yet in spite of these passages, the Upanishads constantly declare that Brahman is the one true object of knowledge and the whole Scripture is'in fact an attempt not perhaps to define, but at least in some sort to characterise and present an idea, and even a detailed idea, of the Brahman.

The inconsistency is more apparent than real. The Brahman in Its ultimate reality is transcendent, absolute, infinite ; but the senses and the intellect, which the senses supply with material, are finite ; speech also is limited by the deficiencies of the intellect ; Brahman must therefore in Its very nature be unknowable to the intellect and beyond the power of speech to describe, — yet only in its ultimate reality, not in Its aspects of manifestations. The Agnostic Scientist also believes that there must be some great ultimate Reality unknown and probably unknowable to man (*ignoramus et ignorabmus*) from which this Universe proceeds and on which all phenomena depend, but his admission of Unknowableness is confined to the ultimate Nature of this supreme End and not to its expression or manifestation in the Universe. The Upanishad, proceeding by a profounder method than material analysis, casts the net of knowledge wider than the modern Agnostic, yet in the end its attitude is much the same ; it differs only in this important respect that it asserts even the ultimate Brahman to be although inexpressible in the terms of finite knowledge, yet realisable and attainable.

INDIVIDUAL. What appears here as man is an individual being of the Divine ; the Divine extended in multiplicity is the Self of all individual existence, *eko vaśi sarvabhutāntarātmā* (Katha Up. II. 2. 12).

INDIVIDUAL SALVATION. Certainly there is an emphasis in the Upanishads increasing steadily as time goes on into an over-emphasis, on the salvation of the individual, on his rejection of the lower cosmic life. This note increases in them as they become later in date, it swells afterwards into the rejection of all cosmic life whatever and that becomes finally in later Hinduism almost the one dominant and all challenging cry. It does not exist in the earlier Vedic revelation where individual salvation is regarded as a means towards a great cosmic victory, the eventual conquest of heaven and earth by the superconscient Truth and Bliss, and those who have achieved the victory in the past are the conscious helpers of their yet battling posterity. If this earlier note is missing in the Upanishads, then — for great as are these scriptures, luminous, profound, sublime in their unsurpassed truth, beauty and power, yet it is only the ignorant soul that will make itself the slave of a book, — then in using them as an aid to knowledge we must insistently call back the earlier missing note, we must seek elsewhere a solution for the word of the riddle that has been ignored. The Upanishad alone of extant scriptures gives us without veil of stinting, with plenitude and a noble catholicity the truth of the Brahman ; its aid to humanity is therefore indispensable. Only, where anything essential is missing, we must go beyond the Upanishads to seek it, — as for instance, when we add to its emphasis on divine knowledge the indispensable ardent emphasis of the later teachings upon divine love and the high emphasis of the Veda upon divine works.

INDRA. Indra is the power of the Mind ; the senses which the life uses for enjoyment are operations of Indra which he conducts for knowledge and all things that Agni has upbuilt and supports and destroys in the universe are Indra's field and the subject of his functioning.

INHABITANT. Each material object contains an outer or form consciousness involved, absorbed in the form, asleep, seeming to be unconsciousness driven by an unknown and unfelt inner Existence, — he who is awake in the sleeper, the universal Inhabitant of the Upanishads.

INTUITIVE POETRY IN THE UPANISHADS. The language of the intuitive thinking moves always to an affinity with poetic speech and in the ancient Upanishads it used that commonly as its natural vehicle. " The Spirit went abroad, a thing pure, bright, unwounded by sin, without body or sinew or scar ; the Seer, the Thinker, the Self-born who breaks into being all around us, decreed of old all things in their nature from long eternal years." " There sun shines not nor moon nor star nor these lightnings blaze nor this fire ; all this world is luminous only with his light."

Are we listening, one might ask, to the voice of poetry or philosophy or religion ? It is all three voices cast in one, indistinguishable in the eternal choir.

INWARD LIFE. There must be for the divine life a transference of the centre and immediate source of dynamic effectuation of the being from out inward ; for there the soul is seated, but it is veiled or half veiled and our immediate being and source of action is for the present on the surface. In men, says the Upanishad, the Self-Existent has cut the doors of consciousness outward, but a few turn the eye inward and it is these who see and know the Spirit and develop the spiritual being. Thus to look into ourselves and see and enter into ourselves and live within is the first necessity for transformation of nature and for the divine life.

ISHA UPANISHAD. The *Iśa* is concerned with the whole problem of the world and life and works and the human destiny in their relation to the supreme truth of the Brahman. It embraces in its brief eighteen verses most of the fundamental problems of Life and scans them swiftly with the idea of the Self and its becomings, the supreme Lord and His workings as the key that shall unlock all gates. The oneness of all existence is its dominating note.

It teaches the reconciliation, by the perception of essential Unity, of the apparently incompatible opposites, God and the World, Renunciation and Enjoyment, Action and internal Freedom, the One and the Many, Being and its Becomings, the passive divine Impersonality and the active divine Personality, the Knowledge and the Ignorance, the Becoming and the Not-Becoming, Life on earth and beyond and the supreme Immortality.

Iśa Up. and Monism : The Isha Upanishad does not teach a pure and exclusive Monism ; it declares the One without denying the Many and its method is to see the One in the Many. It asserts the simultaneous validity of Vidya and Avidya and upholds as the object of action and knowledge an immortality consistent with Life and Birth in this world. It regards every object as itself the universe and every soul as itself, the divine Purusha. The ensemble of these ideas is consistent only with a synthetic or comprehensive as opposed to an illusionist or exclusive Monism.

ISHA UPANISHAD AND THE KENA. Both are concerned with the same grand problem, the winning of the state of Immortality, the relations of the divine all-ruling, all-possessing Brahman to the world and to the human consciousness, the means of passing out of our present state of divided self, ignorance and suffering into the unity, the truth, the divine beatitude. As the Isha closes with the aspiration towards the supreme felicity, so the Kena closes with the definition of Brahman as the Delight and the injunction to worship and seek after That as the Delight.*

The Truth behind Mind, Life, Sense must be that which controls by exceeding it. It is the Lord, the all-possessing Deva. This is the conclusion at which the Isha Upanishad arrives by the synthesis of all existence ; the Kena arrives at it by the antithesis of one governing self-existence to all this that exists variously by another power of being than its own. Each follows its own method for the resolution of all things into the one Reality, but the conclusion is identical. It is the All-possessing and All-enjoying, who is reached by the renunciation of separate being, separate possession and separate delight. But the Isha addresses itself to the awakened seeker ; it begins therefore with the all-inhabiting Lord, proceeds to the all-becoming Self and returns to the Lord as the Self of the cosmic movement, because it has to justify works to the seeker of the Uncreated and to institute a divine life founded on the joy of immortality and on the unified consciousness of the individual

---

* Nevertheless there is a variation in the starting point, even in the standpoint, a certain sensible divergence in the attitude. For the precise subject of the two Upanishads is not identical.
  vide Isha Upanishad ; Kena Upanishad.

made one with the universal. The Kena addresses itself to the world still attracted by the external life, not yet wholly awakened, not wholly a seeker ; it begins therefore with the Brahman as the Self beyond Mind and proceeds to the Brahman as the hidden Lord of all our mental and vital activities, because it has to point this soul upward beyond its apparent and outward existence. But the two opening chapters of the Kena only state less widely from this other view-point the Isha's doctrine of the Self and its becomings ; the last two repeat in other terms of thought the Isha's doctrine of the Lord and His movement.

JĪVANMUKTA. One who lives and is yet released in his inner self from the bondage of phenomenal existence.

JUGUPSĀ. The shrinking of the limited being from that which is not himself and not sympathetic or in harmony with himself, its impulse of self-defence against " others ".
" He who sees everywhere the Self in all existences and all existences in the Self, shrinks not thereafter from aught." (Isha Up. 6)

KAIVALYA. The Being beyond the Highest. It is not *tūriya* who is *śivam, śāntam, advaitam, saccidānandam,* but that which is beyond *śivam* and *aśivam,* good and evil, *śāntam* and *kalilam,* calm and chaos, *dvaitam* and *advaitam,* duality and unity. Sat, Chit and Ananda are in the Highest, but he is neither Sat, Chit nor Ananda nor any combination of these. He is All and yet He is *neti, neti.* He is one and yet He is many. He is Parabrahman and He is Parameshvara. He is male and He is Female. He is *tat* and He is *sah.* This is the Higher than the Highest. He is the Purusha, the Being in whose image the world and all the jivas are made, who pervades all and underlies all the workings of Prakriti as its reality and self.
Path to Kaivalya : Three necessary elements — first, the starting point, right knowledge, implying the escape from Ignorance, from non-knowledge and false knowledge ; next, the process or means, escape from all evil, *i.e.* sin, pain and grief ; last, the goal, Purushottama, the Being who is beyond the Highest, that

5

is, beyond *tūriya*, *tūriya* being the Highest. By the escape from
sin, pain and grief one attains absolute Ananda, the last term
of existence, we reach that in which Ananda exists.

KARMA. "They say indeed that the conscious being is
made of desire. But of whatsoever desire he comes to
be he comes to be of that will, and of whatever will he comes
to be, he does that action, and whatever his action, to (the
result of) that he reaches. . . . Adhered to by his Karma, he
goes in his subtle body to wherever his mind cleaves, then coming to the end of his Karma, even of whatsoever action he does
here, he returns from that world to this world for Karma."
(Brihadaranyaka Up. IV. 4. 5, 6)

In the view expressed in this verse of the Upanishad the
Karma or action of this life is exhausted by life in the world
beyond in which its results are fulfilled and the soul returns to
earth for fresh Karma. The cause of birth in this world, of
Karma, of the soul's passage to other-world existence and its
return here is, throughout, the soul's own consciousness, will
and desire.

"Equipped with qualities, a doer of works and creator of their
consequences, he reaps the result of his actions ; he is the ruler
of the life and he moves in his journey according to his own
acts ; he has idea and ego and is to be known by the qualities
of his intelligence and his quality of self. Smaller than the
hundredth part of the tip of a hair, the soul of the living being
is capable of infinity. Male is he not nor female nor neuter,
but is joined to whatever body he takes as his own." (Shvetashvatara Up. V. 7-10)

KAVI. Indicates the divine supra-intellectual Knowledge
which by direct vision and illumination sees the reality, the
principles and the forms of things in their true relations.

KAVIR MANĪṢĪ. The Lord appears to us in the relative
notion of the process of things first as Kavi, the Wise, the Seer.
The Kavi sees the Truth in itself, the truth in its becoming, in
its essence, possibilities, actuality. He contains all that in the
Idea, the Vijnana, called the Truth and Law, *satyam ṛtam*. He

contains it comprehensively, not piecemeal ; the Truth and Law of things is the *brhat*, the Large. Viewed by itself, the realm of Vijnana would seem a realm of predetermination, of concentration, of compelling seed-state. But it is a determination not in previous Time, but in perpetual Time ; a Fate compelled by the Soul, not compelling it, compelling rather the action and result, present in the expansion of the movement as well as in the concentration of the Idea. Therefore the truth of the Soul is freedom and mastery, not subjection and bondage. Purusha commands Prakriti, Prakriti does not compel Purusha.

The Manishi takes his stand in the possibilities. He has behind him the freedom of the Infinite and brings it in as a background for the determination of the finite. Therefore every action in the world seems to emerge from a balancing and clashing of various possibilities. None of these, however, are effective in the determination except by their secret consonance with the Law of that which has to become. The Kavi is in the Manishi and upholds him in his working. But viewed by itself the realm of the Manishi would seem to be a state of plasticity, of free-will, of the interaction of forces, but of a free-will in thought which is met by a fate in things.

KENA UPANISHAD. The Kena concerns itself with the relation of mind consciousness to Brahman consciousness. The material world and the physical life are taken for granted. But the material world and the physical life exist for us only by virtue of our internal self and our internal life. According as our mental instruments represent to us the external world, according as our vital force in obedience to the mind deals with its impacts and objects, so will be our outward life and existence. The world is for us what our mind and senses declare them to be ; life is what our mentality determines that it shall become. The question is asked by the Upanishad, what then are these mental instruments ? What is this mental life which uses the external ? Are they the last witnesses, the supreme and final power ? Is mind all or is this human existence only a veil of something greater, mightier, more remote and profound than itself ? The Upanishad replies that there is such a greater existence behind, which is to the mind and its instruments, to the life-force and its workings what they are to the material world.

This Brahman consciousness is the Lord and ruler of all the world; the energies of the gods in the mortal consciousness are its energies; when they conquer and grow great it is because Brahman has fought and won. This world therefore is an inferior action, a superficial representation of something infinitely greater, more perfect, more real than itself.

What is that something? It is the All-Bliss which in infinite being and immortal force. It is that pure and utter bliss and not the desires and enjoyments of this world which men ought to worship and to seek. How to seek it is the one question that matters; to follow after it with all one's being is the only truth and the only wisdom.

KNOWLEDGE AND IGNORANCE. Knowledge is the inherent power of consciousness of the timeless, spaceless, unconditioned Self which shows itself in its essence as a unity of being; it is this consciousness that alone is real and complete knowledge because it is an eternal transcendence which is not only self-aware but holds in itself, manifests, originates, determines, knows the temporally eternal successions of the universe. Ignorance is the consciousness of being in the successions of Time, divided in its knowledge by dwelling in the moment, divided in its conception of self-being by dwelling in the divisions of Space and the relations of circumstance, self-prisoned in the multiple working of the unity. It is called the Ignorance because it has put behind it the knowledge of unity and by that very fact is unable to know truly or completely either itself or the world, either the transcendent or the universal reality. Living within the Ignorance, from moment to moment, from field to field, from relation to relation, the conscious soul stumbles on in the error of a fragmentary knowledge. "Living and moving within the Ignorance, they go round and round stumbling and battered, men deluded, like the blind led by one who is blind." (Mundaka Up. I. 2. 8)

"Two are there, hidden in the secrecy of the Infinite, the Knowledge and the Ignorance; but perishable is the Ignorance, immortal is the Knowledge; another than they is He

who rules over both the Knowledge and the Ignorance."
(Shvethashvatara Up. V. 1)

" Into a blind darkness they enter who follow after the
Ignorance, they as if into a greater darkness who devote themselves to the Knowledge alone.

He who knows that as both in one, the Knowledge and the
Ignorance, by the Ignorance crosses beyond death and by the
Knowledge enjoys Immortality." (Isha Up. II. 9, 11)

KNOWLEDGE OF THE SELF. Since the Self which we
come to realise by the Path of Knowledge is not only the reality
which lies behind and supports the states and movements of
our psychological being, but also that transcendent and
universal Existence which has manifested itself in all the
movements of the universal, the knowledge of the Self includes
also the knowledge of the principles of Being, its fundamental
modes and its relations with the principles of the phenomenal
universe. This was what was meant by the Upanishad when it
spoke of the Brahman as that which being known all is known
(*yasmin vijnāte sarvam vijnātam*). It has to be realised first as
the pure principle of Existence, afterwards, says the Upanishad,
its essential modes become clear to the soul which realises it.

KNOWLEDGE SEPARATIVE AND KNOWLEDGE BY
IDENTITY. " Where there is duality, there other sees other,
other hears, touches, thinks of, knows other. But when one
sees all as the Self, by what shall one know it ? It is by the
Self that one knows all this that is. . . . All betrays him who
sees all elsewhere than in the Self ; for all this that is is the
Brahman, all beings and all this that is are this Self."
(Brihadaranyaka Up., IV. 5. 15, 7)

" There is no annihilation of the seeing of the seer, the
speaking of the speaker . . . the hearing of the hearer . . . the
knowing of the knower, for they are indestructible ; but it is
not a second or other than and separate from himself that he
sees, speaks of, hears, knows." (Ibid. IV. 3. 23-30)

KNOWLEDGE-VISION. We may hear clear and luminous
teachings about the Self from philosophers or teachers or from

ancient writings ; we may by thought, inference, imagination, analogy or by any other available means attempt to form a mental figure or conception of it : we may hold firmly that conception in our mind and fix it by an entire and exclusive concentration ; * but we have not yet realised it, we have not seen God. It is only when after long and persistent concentration or by other means the veil of the mind is rent or swept aside, only when a flood of light breaks over the awakened mentality, *jyotirmaya brahman,* and conception gives place to a knowledge-vision in which the Self is as present, real, concrete as a physical object to the physical eye, that we possess in knowledge ; for we have seen.

KNOWN AND UNKNOWN. The known is all that we grasp and possess by our present mentality ; it is all that is not the supreme Brahman but only form and phenomenon of it to our sense and mental cognition. The unknown is that which is beyond the known and though unknown, is not unknowable, if we can enlarge our faculties or attain to others that we do not yet possess.

KSARA PURUSA. The Self reflecting the changes and movements of Nature, participating in them, immersed in the consciousness of the movement and seeming in it to be born and die, increase and diminish, progress and change. Atman, as the *ksara,* enjoys change and division and duality ; controls secretly its own changes but seems to be controlled by them ; enjoys the oppositions of pleasure and pain, good and bad, but appears to be their victim ; possesses and upholds the action of Nature, by which it seems to be created.

KRATU. The Vedic term *kratu* means sometimes the action itself, sometimes the effective power behind action represented in mental consciousness by the will. Agni is this power. He is divine force which manifests first in Matter as heat and light and material energy and then, taking different forms in the other

---

* This is the idea of the triple operation of Jnanayoga, *sravana, manana, nididhyasana,* hearing, thinking or mentalising and fixing in concentration.

principles of man's consciousness, leads him by a progressive manifestation upwards to the Truth and Bliss.

LAW. Every object holds in itself the law of its own being eternally, *śāśvathībyaḥ samābhyaḥ*, from years sempiternal, in perpetual Time. All relations in the totality of objects are thus determined by their Inhabitant, the Self-existent, the Self-becoming, and stand contained in the nature of things by the omnipresence of the One, the Lord, by His self-vision which is their inherent subjective Truth, by His self-becoming which against a background of boundless possibilities, is the Law of their inevitable evolution in the objective Fact.

Therefore all things are arranged by Him perfectly, *yāthātathyataḥ*, as they should be in their nature. There is an imperative harmony in the All, which governs the apparent discords of individualisation. That discord would be real and operate in eternal chaos, if there were only a mass of individual forms and forces, if each form and force did not contain in itself and were not in its reality the self-existent All, the Lord.

This is the nature of Law or Truth in the world that it is the just working and bringing out of that which is contained in being, implied in the essence and nature of the thing itself, latent in its self-being and self-law, *svabhāva* and *svadharma*, as seen by the divine Knowledge. To use one of those wonderful formulas of the Upanishad which contain a world of knowledge in a few revealing words, it is the Self-existent who as the seer and thinker becoming everywhere has arranged in Himself all things rightly from years eternal according to the truth of that which they are. (Isha Up. 8)

LAW OF THE TRUTH. We must learn to see things as they are, see ourselves as we are. Our present action is one in which self-knowledge and will are divided. We start with a fundamental falsehood, that we have a separate existence from others and we try to know the relations of separate beings in their separateness and act on the knowledge so formed for an individual utility. The law of the Truth would work in us if we saw the totality of our existence containing all others, its forms created by the action of the totality, its powers working

in and by the action of the totality. Our internal and external
action would then well naturally and directly out of our self-
existence, out of the very truth of things and not in obedience
to an intermediate principle which is in its nature a falsifying
reflection.

LEARNING AND BRAHMAN. *Vide* Grace.

LIBERATION. " To dwell in our true being is liberation."
(Mahopanishad, V. 2)

LIFE — ITS SIGNIFICANCE. In the Vedanta of the
Upanishads, the Becoming of Brahman is accepted as a reality ;
there is room therefore for a truth of the becoming : there is in
that truth a right law of life, a permissible satisfaction of the
hedonistic element in our being, its delight of temporal
existence, an effective utilisation of its practical energy, of the
executive force of consciousness in it.

LIGHT AND SHADE. " There are two that drink deep of
the truth in the world of work well accomplished : they are
lodged in the secret plane of being, in the highest kingdom of
the most High : as of light and shade the knowers of Brahman
speak of them." (Katha Up. I. 3. 1)

LOGIC OF BRAHMAN. " He is subtler than subtlety and
that which logic cannot reach. This wisdom is not to be had
by reasoning." (Katha Up. I. 2. 8, 9)

LOGICAL REASON AND UPANISHADS. The sages of
the Veda and Vedanta relied entirely upon intuition and spiritual experience. It is by an error that scholars sometimes speak
of great debates or discussions in the Upanishad. Wherever
there is the appearance of a controversy, it is not by discussion,
by dialectics or the use of logical reasoning that it proceeds,
but by a comparison of intuitions and experiences in which the
less luminous gives place to the more luminous, the narrower,
faultier or less essential to the more comprehensive, more
perfect, more essential. The question asked by one thinker

of another is " What dost thou know ? ", not " What dost thou think ? ", nor " To what conclusion has thy reasoning arrived ? ". Nowhere in the Upanishads do we find any trace of logical reasoning urged in support of the truths of Vedanta. Intuition, the sages seem to have held, must be corrected by a more perfect intuition ; logical reasoning cannot be its judge.

LORD. " It is He that has gone abroad — That which is bright, bodiless, without scar of imperfection, without sinews, pure, unpierced by evil. The Seer, the Thinker, the One who becomes everywhere, the Self-existent has ordered objects perfectly according to their nature from years sempiternal." (Isha Up. 8)

LORD AND SHAKTI. " It is the might of the Godhead in the world that turns the wheel of Brahman. Him one must know, the supreme Lord of all lords, the supreme Godhead above all godheads. Supreme too is his Shakti and manifold the natural working of her knowledge and her force. One Godhead, occult in all beings, the inner Self of all beings, the all-pervading, absolute without qualities, the overseer of all actions, the witness, the knower." (Shvetashvatara Up. VI. 1 7, 8, 11)

LOVE. The Vedic seers looked at Love from above, from its source and root and saw it and received it in their humanity as an outflowing of the divine Delight. The Taittiriya Upanishad expounding this spiritual and cosmic bliss of the godhead, Vedantic Ananda, Vedic Mayas, says of it, " Love is its head." But the word it chooses for Love, *priyam*, means properly the delightfulness of the objects of the soul's inner pleasure and satisfaction. The Vedic singers used the same psychology. They couple *mayas* and *prayas*, — *mayas*, the principle of inner felicity independent of all objects, *prayas*, its outflowing as the delight and pleasure of the soul in objects and beings. The Vedic happiness is this divine felicity which brings with it the boon of a pure possession and sinless pleasure in all things founded upon the unfailing touch of the Truth and Right in the freedom of a large universality.

Only when the heart, the will and the mind of knowledge associate themselves with the law of sacrifice and gladly follow it, can there come the deep joy and the happy fruitfulness of divine sacrifice. The mind's knowledge of the law and the heart's gladness in it culminate in the perception that it is to our own Self and Spirit and the one Self and the Spirit of all that we give. And this is true even when our self-offering is still to our fellow creatures or to lesser Powers and Principles and not yet to the Supreme. " Not for the sake of the wife ", says Yajnavalkya in the Upanishad, " but for the sake of the Self is the wife dear to us." This in the lower sense of the individual self is the hard fact behind the coloured and passionate professions of egoistic love ; but in a higher sense it is the inner significance of that love too which is not egoistic but divine. All true love and all sacrifice are in their essence Nature's contradiction of the primary egoism and its separative error ; it is her attempt to turn from a necessary first fragmentation towards a recovered oneness. All unity between creatures is in its essence a self-finding, a fusion with that from which we have separated and a discovery of one's self in others.

LOWER SACRIFICES. " ' Come with us ', ' Come with us ', they cry to him, these luminous fires of sacrifice and they bear him by the rays of the sun speaking to him pleasant words of sweetness, doing him homage, ' This is your holy world of Brahman and the heaven of your righteousness.' But frail are the ships of sacrifice, frail these forms of sacrifice, all the eighteen of them, in which are declared the lower works ; fools are they who hail them as the highest good and they come yet again to this world of age and death. They dwell in many bonds of the Ignorance, children thinking, ' We have achieved our aim of Paradise ' ; for when the men of works are held by their affections, and arrive not at the Knowledge, then they are overtaken by anguish, then their Paradise wastes by enjoying and they fall from their heavens. Minds bewildered who hold the oblation offered and the well dug for the greatest righteousness and know not any other highest good, on the back of heaven they enjoy the world won by their righteousness and enter again this or even a lower world." (Mundaka Up. I. 2. 6, 7, 9 and 10)

MAHACHAMASYA. *Vide* Vyahritis.

MAHARLOKA. Between the two creations (the higher and the lower), linking them together, is the world or organisation of consciousness of which the infinite Truth of things is the foundation. There dominant individualisation no longer usurps the all-pervading soul and the foundation of consciousness is its own vast totality arranging in itself individualised movements which never lose the consciousness of their integrality and total oneness with all others. Multiplicity no longer prevails and divides, but even in the complexity of its movements always refers back to essential unity and its own integral totality. This world is therefore called Maharloka or world of large consciousness.

Mahat, Vijnana, is not the supreme plane of our consciousness but a middle or link plane. Interposed between the triune glory of the utter Spirit, the infinite existence, consciousness and bliss of the Eternal and our lower triple being and nature, it is as if it stood there as the mediating, formulated, organising and creative wisdom, power and joy of the Eternal.

MANIFESTATION. " This whole world is filled with beings who are His members." (Shvetashvatara Up. IV. 10)
" This is That, the Truth of things : as from one high-kindled fire thousands of different sparks are born and all have the same form of fire, so, O fair son, from the immutable manifold becomings are born and even into that they depart." (Mundaka Up., II. 1. 1)
" As the spider puts out and gathers in, as herbs spring up upon the earth, as hair of head and body grow from a living man, so here all is born from the Immutable. (Mundaka Up. I. 1. 7)

MANĪṢī. Indicates the labouring mentality, which works from the divided consciousness through the possibilities of

things downward to the actual manifestation in form and upward
to their reality in the self-existent Brahman.
Vide Kavir Manīsī.

MANOBRAHMA. " He knew mind for the Eternal. For
from mind alone, it appears, are these creatures born and being
born they live by mind, and to mind they go hence and return."
(Taittiriya Up. III. 4)

MANOMAYA ĀTMĀ. " There is yet a second and inner
Self which is other than this that is of Prana, and it is made of
Mind. And the Self of Mind fills the Self of Prana. Now the
Self of Mind is made in the image of a man ; according as is
the human image of the other, so is it in the image of the
man. Yajur is the head of him and the Rigveda is his right
side and the Samaveda is his left side : the Commandment is
his spirit which is the self of him, Atharvan Angiras is his
lower member whereon he rests abidingly." (Taittiriya Up.
II. 3)
" This Self of Mind is the soul in the body to the former one
which was of Prana." (Taittiriya Up. II. 4)

MANOMAYA PURUṢA. The Spirit poised in mind
becomes the mental self of a mental world and dwells there in
the reign of its own pure and luminous mental Nature. There
it acts in the intense freedom of the cosmic Intelligence
supported by the combined workings of a psycho-mental and
higher emotional mind-force, subtilised and enlightened by the
clarity and happiness of the sattwic principle proper to the
mental existence. In the individual the spirit so poised becomes
a mental soul, *manomaya puruṣa,* in whose nature the clarity
and luminous power of the mind acts in its own right independent of any limitation or oppression by the vital or corpo-
real instruments ; it rather rules and determines entirely the
forms of its body and the powers of its life. For mind in its
own plane is not limited by life and obstructed by matter as it
is here in the earth-process. This mental soul lives in a mental
or subtle body which enjoys capacities of knowledge, perception, sympathy and interpenetration with other beings hardly

imaginable by us and a free, delicate and extensive mentalised sense-faculty not limited by the grosser conditions of the life nature or the physical nature.

MĀTARISVAN. He who extends himself in the Mother or the container — whether that be the containing mother element Ether, or the material energy called Earth in the Veda and spoken of there as the Mother. It is a Vedic epithet of the God Vayu, who, representing the divine principle in the Life-energy, Prana, extends himself in Matter and vivifies its forms. It signifies the divine Life-power that presides in all forms of cosmic activity.

MĀYĀ. Signifying originally in the Veda comprehensive and creative knowledge, Wisdom that is from of old; afterwords taken in its second and derivative sense, cunning, magic, Illusion. In this second significance it can really be appropriate to the workings of the lower Nature which has put behind it the Divine Wisdom and is absorbed in the experiences of the separative Ego.

" The Master of Maya creates this world by his Maya and within it is confined another ; one should know his Maya as Nature and the Master of Maya as the great Lord of all." (Shvetashvatara Up. IV. 9. 10)

MEMORY. "Memory is greater — without memory men could think and know nothing. . . . As far as goes the movement of Memory, there he ranges at will." (Chhandogya Up. VII. 13)

MENTAL BEING — LIMITATIONS IN SELF-PERFEC-TION. Mind indeed can never be a perfect instrument of the Spirit ; a supreme self-expression is not possible in its movements because to separate, divide, limit is its very character. Even if mind could be free from all positive falsehood and error, even if it could be all intuitive and infallibly intuitive, it could still present and organise only half-truths or separate truths and these too not in their own body but in luminous representative figures put together to make an accumulated total or a massed structure. Therefore the self-perfecting mental being here must either depart into pure spirit by the shedding of its lower existence or return upon the physical life to develop in it a capacity not yet found in our mental and psychic nature. This is what the Upanishad expresses when it says that the heavens attained by the mind Purusha are those to which man is lifted by the rays of the sun, the diffused, separated, though intense beams of the supramental truth consciousness, and from these it has to return to the earthly existence. But the illuminates who renouncing earth-life go beyond through the gateways of the sun, do not return hither. The mental being exceeding his sphere does not return because by that transition he enters a high range of existence peculiar to the superior hemisphere. He cannot bring down its greater spiritual nature into this lower triplicity ; for here the mental being is the highest expression of the Self. Here the triple mental, vital and physical body provides almost the whole range of our capacity and cannot suffice for that greater consciousness ; the vessel has not been built to contain a greater godhead or to house the splendours of this supramental force and knowledge.

This limitation is true only so long as man remains closed within the boundaries of the mental Maya.

MENTAL LEADER.   What is it that reflects and accepts the mutable personality, since the Self is immutable ? We have in fact, an immutable Self, a real Person, lord of this ever-changing personality which, again, assumes ever-changing bodies, but the real Self knows itself as above the mutation, watches and enjoys it, but is not involved in it.   Through what does it enjoy the changes and feel them to be its own, even knowing itself to be unaffected by them ?   The mind and ego-sense are only inferior instruments ; there must be some more essential form of itself which the Real Man puts forth, puts in front of itself, as it were, and at the back of the changings to support and mirror them without being actually changed by them. This more essential form is the mental being or mental person which the Upanishads speak of as the mental leader of the life and body, *manomayaḥ praṇaśarira-neta.* It is that which maintains the ego-sense as a function in the mind and enables us to have the

firm conception of continuous identity in Time as opposed to
the timeless identity of Self.

MIND. Mind was called by Indian psychologists the eleventh
and ranks as the supreme sense. In the ancient arrangement
of the senses, five of knowledge and five of action, it was the
sixth of the organs of knowledge and at the same time the sixth
of the organs of action. It is a common-place of psychology
that the effective functioning of the senses of knowledge is
inoperative without the assistance of the mind ; the eye may
see, the ear may hear, all the senses may act, but if the mind
pays no attention, the man has not heard, seen, felt, touched or
tasted. Similarly, according to psychology, the organs of action
act only by the force of the mind operating as will or, physio-
logically, by the reactive nervous force from the brain which
must be according to materialistic notions the true self and
essence of all will. In any case, the senses or all senses, if
there are other than the ten, — according to a text in the Upanishad there should be at least fourteen, seven and seven, —
all senses appear to be only organisations, functionings, instru-
mentations of the mind-consciousness, devices which it has
formed in the course of its evolution in living matter.

Modern psychology has extended our knowledge and has
admitted us to a truth which the ancients already knew but
expressed in other language. We know now or we rediscover
the truth that the conscious operation of mind is only a surface
action. There is a much vaster and more potent subconscious
mind which loses nothing of what the senses bring to it ; it
keeps all its wealth in an inexhaustible store of memory, *akṣitam
śravaḥ*. The surface mind may pay no attention, still the subconscious mind attends, receives, treasures up with an infallible
accuracy. The illiterate servant-girl hears daily her master
reciting Hebrew in his study ; the surface mind pays no attention to the unintelligible gibberish but the sub-conscious mind
hears, remembers and, when in an abnormal condition it comes
up to the surface, reproduces those learned recitations with a
portentous accuracy which the most correct and retentive
scholar might envy. The man or mind has not heard because
he did not attend ; the greater man or mind within has heard

because he always attends, or rather sub-tends, with an infinite capacity. So too a man put under an anaesthetic and operated upon has felt nothing ; but release his subconscious mind by hypnosis and he will relate accurately every detail of the operation and its appropriate sufferings ; for the stupor of the physical sense-organ could not prevent the larger mind within from observing and feeling.

Similarly we know that a large part of our physical action is instinctive and directed not by the surface but by the subconscious mind. And we know now that it is a mind that acts and not merely an ignorant nervous reaction from the brute physical brain. The subconscious mind in the catering insect knows the anatomy of the beetle it intends to immobilise and make food for its young and it directs the sting accordingly, as unerringly as the most skilful surgeon, provided the mere limited surface mind with its groping and faltering nervous action does not get in the way and falsify the inner knowledge or the inner will-force.

Mind in Dream :   " The Mind in dream revels in the glory of his imaginings. All that it has seen it seems to see over again, and of all that it has heard it repeats the hearing : yea, all that it has felt and thought and known in many lands and in various regions, these it lives over again in its dreaming. What it has seen and what it has not seen, what it has heard and what it has not heard, what it has known and what it has not known, what is and what is not, all, all it sees : for the Mind is the Universe." (Prashna Up. IV. 5)

MORTAL MAN.   " Mortal man withers like the fruits of the field and like the fruits of the field he is born again." Katha Up. I. 1. 6)

MYSTERY.   " One unmoving that is swifter than Mind, That the Gods reach not, for It progresses ever in front. That, standing, passes beyond others as they run. That moves and That moves not ; That is far and the same is near ; That is within all this and That also is outside all this." (Isha Up. 4, 5)

MYSTICS OF THE VEDANTA. The early Vedantists were mystics not in the sense of being vague and loose-thoughted visionaries, but in the sense of being intuitional symbolists — men who regarded the world as a movement of consciousness and all material forms and energies as external symbols and shadows of deeper and deeper internal realities.

NĀDĪ. " A hundred and one are the nerves of the heart, and of all these only one issues out through the head of a man : by this his soul mounts up to its immortal home, but the rest lead him to all sorts and conditions of births in his passing." (Katha Up. II. 3. 16)

NAME AND FORM. Our conception of the infinite is formlessness, but everywhere we see form and forms surrounding us and it can be and is affirmed of the Divine Being that he is at once Form and the Formless. For here too the apparent contradiction does not correspond to a real opposition ; the Formless is not a negation of the power of formation, but the condition for the Infinite's free formation : for otherwise there would be a single Form or only a fixity or sum of possible forms in a finite universe. The formlessness is the character of the spiritual essence, the spirit-substance of the Reality ; all finite realities are powers, forms, self-shapings of that substance : the Divine is formless and nameless, but by that very reason capable of manifesting all possible names and shapes of being. Forms are manifestations, not arbitrary inventions out of nothing ; for line and colour, mass and design which are the essentials of form carry always in them a significance, are, it might be said, secret values and significances of an unseen reality made visible ; it is for that reason that figure, line, hue, mass, composition can embody what would be otherwise unseen, can convey what would be otherwise occult to the sense. Form may be said to be the innate body, the inevitable self-revelation of the formless, and this is true not only of external shapes, but of the unseen formations of mind and life which we seize only by our thought and those sensible forms of which only the subtle grasp of the inner consciousness can become aware. Name in its deeper sense is not the word by which we describe the object, but the total

6

power, quality, character of the reality which a form of things embodies and which we try to sum up by a designating sound, a knowable name, *Nomen*. *Nomen* in this sense, we might say, is *Numen* ; the secret Names of the Gods are their power, quality, character of being caught up by the consciousness and made conceivable. The Infinite is nameless, but in that namelessness all possible names, Numens of the Gods, the names and forms of all realities, are already envisaged and prefigured, because they are there latent and inherent in the All-Existence.

" He who is the Omniscient, the All-wise, He whose energy is all made of knowledge, from Him is born this that is Brahman here, this Name and Form and Matter." (Mundaka Up. I. I. 9)

" The Eternal Father desired children, therefore he put forth his energy and by the heat of his energy produced twin creatures, Prana the Life, who is Male, and Rayi the Matter, who is Female. ' These ', said he, ' shall make for me children of many natures.' The Sun verily is Life and the Moon is no more than Matter : yet truly all this Universe formed and formless is Matter : therefore Form and Matter are One." (Prashna Up. I. 4-5)

NECKLACE OF MANY FIGURES. Prakriti, creative Nature which comes under the control of the soul that has attained to the divine existence. (Katha Up. I. 1. 16)

NETI, NETI. The traditional way of knowledge eliminates individual and universe. The Absolute it seeks after is featureless, indefinable, relationless, not this, not that, *neti; neti.*

Brahman is the One besides whom there is nothing else existent. But this unity is in its nature indefinable. When we seek to envisage it by the mind we are compelled to proceed through an infinite series of conceptions and experiences. And yet in the end we are obliged to negate our largest conceptions, our most comprehensive experiences in order to affirm that the Reality exceeds all definitions. We arrive at the formula of the Indian sages, *neti neti,* " It is not this, It is not that " ; there is no experience by which we can limit It, there is no conception by which It can be defined.

The ancient sages spoke indeed of Brahman negatively, — they said of it, *neti, neti,* it is not this, it is not that, — but they took care also to speak of it positively ; they said of it too, it is this, it is that, it is all : for they saw that to limit it either by positive or negative definitions was to fall away from its truth.

NON-BEING. " In the beginning all this was the Non-Being. It was thence that Being was born." (Taittiriya Up. II. 7)

We really mean by this Nothing something beyond the last term to which we can reduce our purest conception and our most abstract or subtle experience of actual being as we know or conceive it while in this universe. This Nothing is merely a something beyond positive conception. We erect a fiction of nothingness in order to overpass, by the method of total exclusion, all that we can know and consciously are. Actually it is a zero which is All or an indefinable Infinite which appears to the mind a blank, because mind grasps only finite constructions, but is in fact the only true Existence.

Another Upanishad rejects the birth of Being out of Non-Being as an impossibility ; Being, it says, can only be born from Being. But if we take Non-Being in the sense, not of an inexistent Nihil but of an *x* which exceeds our idea or experience of existence, — a sense applicable to the Absolute Brahman of the Advaita as well as the Void or Zero of the Buddhists, the impossibility disappears, for That may very well be the source of Being, whether by a conceptual or formative Maya or a manifestation or creation out of itself.

OM. The foundation of all the potent creative sounds of the revealed word ; Om is the one universal formulation of the energy of sound and speech, that which contains and sums up, synthetises and releases, all the spiritual power and all the potentiality of *Vāk* and *Śabda* and of which the other sounds, out of whose stuff words of speech are woven, are supposed to be the developed evolutions.

All word and thought are an outflowering of the great Om, — Om, the Word, the Eternal. Manifest in the form of sensible objects, manifest in that conscious play of creative self-

conception of which forms and objects are the figures, manifest
behind in the self-gathered superconscient power of the Infinite,
Om is the sovereign source, seed, womb of thing and idea, form
and name, — it is itself, integrally, the supreme Intangible, the
original Unity, the timeless Mystery self-existent above all manifestation in supernal being.

Aum :   A, the spirit of the gross and external, Virat, U, the
spirit of the subtle and internal, Taijasa, M, the spirit of the
secret superconscient omnipotence, Prajna, Om the Absolute,
Turiya.

"OM is this imperishable Word, OM is the Universe, and
this is the exposition of OM. The past, the present and the
future, all that was, all that is, all that will be, is OM. Likewise all else that may exist beyond the bounds of Time, that
too is OM." (Mandukya Up. I)

"By Om the triple knowledge proceeds ; with Om the priest
recites the Rik, with Om he pronounces the Yajur, with Om he
chants the Sama. And all this is for the heaping of the Imperishable and by the greatness of It and the Delightfulness.
(Chhandogya Up. I. 1. 9)

"OM is the Eternal, OM is all this universe. OM is the
syllable of assent : saying, 'OM ! let us hear,' they begin the
citation. With OM they sing the hymns of the Sama ; with
OM SHOM they pronounce the Shastrā. With OM the priest
officiating at the sacrifice says the response. With OM Brahma
begins creation. With OM one sanctions the burnt offering,
With OM the Brahmin ere he expound the Knowledge, cries
'May I attain the Eternal.' The Eternal verily he attains."
(Taittiriya Up. I. 8)

"Meditate on the Self as OM and happy be your passage
to the other shore beyond the darkness." (Mundaka Up.
II. 2. 6)

Meditations on OM : " If he meditate on the one letter of OM
the syllable, by that enlightened he attains swiftly in the material
universe, and the hymns of the Rigveda escort him to the world
of men : there endowed with askesis and faith and holiness he
experiences majesty. If by the two letters of the syllable he in
the mind attains, to the skies he is exalted and the hymns of the
Yajur escort him to the Lunar World. In the heavens of the

Moon he feels his soul's majesty : then once more he returns. But he who by all the three letters meditates by this syllable, even by OM on the Most High Being, he in the Solar World of light and energy is secured in his attainings : as a snake casts off its slough, so he casts off sin, and the hymns of the Samaveda escort him to the heaven of the Spirit. He from that Lower who is the density of existence beholds the Higher than the Highest of whom every form is one city. Children of death are the letters when they are used as three, the embracing and the inseparable letters." (Prashna Up. V. 3-6)

OM THE ESSENCE. "Earth is the substantial essence of all these creatures and the waters are the essence of earth ; herbs of the field are the essence of the waters, man is the essence of the herbs. Speech is the essence of man, Rig Veda the essence of Speech, Sama the essence of Rik. Of Sama Om is the essence.

This is the eighth essence of the essences and the really essential, the highest and it belongs to the upper hemisphere of things." (Chhandogya Up., I. 1. 2, 3)

OM THE GOAL. "The seat or goal that all the Vedas glorify and which austerities declare, for the desire of which men practise holy living, — Om is that goal.

For this syllable is Brahman, this Syllable is the Most High ; this Syllable if one knows, whatsoever one shall desire, it is his.

This support is the best, this support is the highest, knowing this support one grows great in the world of Brahman." (Katha Up. I. 2. 15-17)

OM THE WORD OF ASSENT. "Om is the syllable of Assent ; for to whatsoever one assents, one says Om ; and assent is blessing of increase. Verily, he becomes a blesser and increaser of the desires of men who with this knowledge worships Om the eternal syllable." (Chhandogya Up. I. 1. 8)

OM AND BRAHMAN. "This imperishable Word that is OM is the Higher Brahman and also the Lower. Therefore the

wise man, by making his home in the Word, wins to one of
these." (Prasna Up. V. 2)

OM, Symbol of Brahman :   *Om* is the symbol and the thing
symbolised.   It is this symbol, *akṣaram*, the syllable in which
all sound of speech is brought back to its wide, pure, indeter-
minate state ; it is the symbolised, *akṣaram*, the changeless,
undiminishing, unincreasing, unappearing, undying Reality which
shows itself to experience in all these changes, increase, dimuni-
tion, appearance, departure which in a particular sum and
harmony of them we call the world, just as *Om* the pure, eternal
sound-basis of speech shows itself to the ear in the variations
and combinations of impure sound which in a particular sum
and harmony of them we call the Veda.   We are to follow after
this *Om* with all our souls, *upāsita*, to apply ourselves to it and
devote ourselves to its knowledge and possession, but always to
Om as the *Udgītha*.

OM AND DESIRES.   " Speech is Rik, Breath is Sama ; the
Imperishable is Om of Udgitha.   These are the divine lovers,
Speech and Breath, Rik and Sama.

As a pair of lovers are these and they cling together in Om
the eternal syllable ; but now when the beloved and her lover
meet, verily, they gratify each the desire of the other.

He becomes a gratifier of the desires of men who with this
knowledge worships Om the eternal syllable." (Chhandogya
Up. I. 1. 5-7)

OM AND IMMORTALITY.   " To the earth the Rigveda
leads, to the skies the Yajur, but the Sama to That which
the sages know.   Thither the wise man by resting on OM
the syllable attains, even to that Supreme Quietude where
age is not and fear is cast out by immortality." (Prashna
Up. V. 7)

OM AND SELF.   " Now this the Self, as the imperishable
Word, is OM : and as to the letters, His parts are the letters
and the letters are His parts, namely, A U M.   The Waker,
Vaishwanara, the Universal Male, He is A, the first letter,
because of Initiality and Pervasiveness : he that knows Him for

such pervades and attains all his desires : he becomes the source
and first. The Dreamer, Taijasa, the Inhabitant in Luminous
Mind, He is U, the second letter, because of Advance and
Centrality : he that knows Him for such, advances the bounds
of his knowledge and rises above difference : nor of his seed is
any born that knows not the Eternal. The Sleeper, Prajna, the
Lord of Wisdom, He is M, the third letter, because of Measure
and Finality : he that knows Him for such measures with himself the Universe and becomes the departure into the Eternal.
Letterless is the fourth, the Incommunicable, the end of phenomena, the Good, the One than Whom there is no other : thus
is OM. He that knows is the Self and enters by his self into the
Self, he that knows, he that knows." (Mandukya Up. 8-12)

ONE SEED. The seed of all is one, — again the great intuition
of the Upanishads foreruns the conclusions of the physical
enquiry, one seed which the universal self-existence by process
of force has disposed in many ways, *ekam bījam bahudhā
śakti-yogāt.*

ONE SELF. The universal Self is not different from the
perceptive and creative, nor the perceptive from the causal,
nor the causal from the Absolute, but it is one " Self-being
which has become all becomings," and which is not any other
than the Lord who manifests Himself as all these individual
existences nor the Lord any other than the sole-existing Brahman
who verily is all this that we can see, sense, live or mentalise.

ONE SPIRIT. " One calm and controlling Spirit within all
creatures that makes one form into many fashions : the calm and
strong who see Him in their self as in a mirror, theirs is eternal
felicity and it is not for others.
The One eternal in the transient, the one consciousness in many
conscious beings, who being One orders the desires of many ;
the calm and strong who behold Him in their self as in a
mirror, theirs is eternal peace and 'tis not for others." (Katha
Up. II. 2. 12-13)
" Even as one Fire has entered into the world, but it shapes
itself to the forms it meets, so there is one Spirit within all

creatures, but it shapes itself to form and form : it is likewise outside these.

Even as one Air has entered into the world but it shapes itself to forms it meets, so there is one Spirit within all creatures, but it shapes itself to form and form ; it is likewise outside these.

Even as the Sun is the eye of all this world, yet is not soiled by the outward blemishes of the visual, so there is one Spirit within all creatures, but the sorrow of this world soils it not : for it is beyond grief and danger." (Katha Up., II. 2. 9-11)

ONENESS AND JOY.   By the integral knowledge we unify all things in the One. We take up all the chords of the universal music, strains sweet or discordant, luminous in their suggestion or obscure, powerful or faint, heard or suppressed, and find them all changed and reconciled in the indivisible harmony of Sachchidananda.   The knowledge brings also the Power and the Joy. " How shall he be deluded, when shall he have sorrow who sees everywhere oneness ? " (Isha Up. 7)

OPENING LINES OF UPANISHADS.   These opening lines or passages are always of great importance ; they are always so designed as to suggest or even sum up, if not all that comes afterwards, yet the essential and pervading idea of the Upanishad. The *īśāvāsyam* of the Vajasaneyi, the *kenesitam manas* of the Talavakara, the Sacrificial Horse of the Brihad Aranyaka, the solitary Atman with its hints of the future world vibrations in the Aitareya are of this type.   The Chhandogya, we see from its first and introductory sentences, is to be a work on the right and perfect way devoting oneself to the Brahman ; the spirit, the methods, formulae are to be given to us.

PARA PURUSA (OR *PURUSOTTAMA*):   The Self containing and enjoying both the stillness and the movement, but conditioned and limited by neither of them. It is the Lord, Brahman, the All, the Indefinable and Unknowable.

PARĀ VIDYĀ AND *APARĀ*.   The higher knowledge and the lower.   There is the supreme supra-intellectual knowledge which concentrates itself on the discovery of the One and Infinite in its transcendence or tries to penetrate by intuition, contemplation, direct inner contact into the ultimate truths behind the appearances of Nature ; there is the lower science which diffuses itself in an outward knowledge of phenomena, the disguises of the One and Infinite as it appears to us in and through the more exterior forms of the world-manifestation around us.

" Twofold is the knowledge that must be known of which the knowers of the Brahman tell, the higher and the lower know-ledge. Of which the lower, the Rig Veda and the Yajur Veda, and the Sama Veda and the Atharva Veda, chanting, ritual, grammar, etymological interpretation, and prosody and astro-nomy. And then the higher by which is known the Immutable." (Mundaka Up. I. 1. 4-5)

PARAMAM DHĀMA. " He knows this supreme Brahman as the highest abiding place in which shines out, inset, the radiant world." (Mundaka Up. III. 2. 1)

PARAMEṢṬHI. The Lord Parameshthi is Brahma — not the creator Hiranyagarbha, but the soul who in this *kalpa* has climbed up to be the instrument of creation, the first in time of the Gods, the *pitāmaha* or original and general Prajapati ; the *pitāmaha*, because all the fathers or special Prajapatis, Daksha and others, are his mind-born children. The confusion between the grandsire and the Creator, who is also called Brahma, is common ; but the distinction is clear. Thus in the Mundaka Upanishad, *brahmā devānam prathamaḥ sambabhūva*, it is the first of Gods, the earliest birth of Time, the father of Atharva, and not the unborn eternal Hiranyagarbha. In the Puranas Brahma is described as in fear of his life from Madhu and Kaitabha, and cannot be the fearless and immortal Hiranya-garbha. Nor would it be possible for Asvalayana (*Kaivalya Up.*) to come to Hiranyagarbha and say " Teach me, Lord," for Hiranyagarbha has no form, nor is He approachable nor does He manifest Himself to man as Shiva and Vishnu do. He is millionfold, Protean, intangible, and for that reason He places in each cycle a Brahma or divine Man between Him and the search and worship of men. It is Brahma or divine Man who is called Parameshthi — or one full of *paramestham*, that which is superlative and highest, — Hiranyagarbha. The power of Hiranyagarbha is in Brahma and creates through him the *nāma* and *rūpa* of things in this cycle.

PARĀRDHA AND *APARĀRDHA*. A separation, acute in practice though unreal in essence, divides the total being of man, the microcosm, as it divides also the world-being the macrocosm. Both have a higher and lower hemisphere, the *parārdha* and *aparārdha* of the ancient wisdom. The higher hemisphere is the perfect and eternal reign of the Spirit ; for there it manifests without cessation or diminution its infinities, deploys the unconcealed glories of its illimitable existence, its illimitable consciousness and knowledge, its illimitable force and power, its illimitable beatitude. The lower hemisphere belongs equally to the Spirit ; but here it is veiled, closely, thickly, by its inferior self-expression of limiting mind, confined life and dividing body. The Self in the lower hemisphere is shrouded in name and form ; its consciousness is broken up by the division between the internal and external, the individual and universal ; its vision and sense are turned outward ; its force, limited by division of consciousness, works in fetters ; its knowledge, will, power, delight, divided by this division, limited by this limitation, are open to the experience of their contrary or perverse forms, to ignorance, weakness and suffering.

PARTIAL TRUTHS. In considering the action of the Infinite we have to avoid the error of the disciple who thought of himself as the Brahman, refused to obey the warning of the elephant-driver to budge from the narrow path and was taken up by the elephant's trunk and removed out of the way ; " You are no doubt the Brahman," said the master to his bewildered disciple, " but why did you not obey the driver Brahman and get out of the path of the elephant Brahman ? "

We must not commit the mistake of emphasising one side of the Truth and concluding from it or acting upon it to the exclusion of all other sides and aspects of the Infinite. The

realisation " I am That " is true, but we cannot safely proceed
on it unless we realise also that all is That.

PATH.   " Long and narrow is the ancient Path, — I have
touched it, I have found it, — the Path by which the wise,
knowers of the Eternal, attaining to salvation, depart hence to
the high world of Paradise." (Brihadaranyaka Up. IV. 4. 8)

PENETRATION INTO THE IMMUTABLE.   " Take up
the bow of the Upanishad, that mighty weapon, set to it an
arrow sharpened by adoration, draw the bow with a heart
wholly devoted to the contemplation of That, and O fair son,
penetrate into that as thy target, even into the Immutable. OM
is the bow and the soul is the arrow, and That, even the
Brahman, is spoken of as the target. That must be pierced with
an unfaltering aim ; one must be absorbed into That as an
arrow is lost in its target." (Mundaka Up. II. 2. 3-4)

PENTADS IN CREATION.   " Earth, sky, heaven, the quarters and the lesser quarters ; fire, air, sun, moon and the constel-
lations ; waters, herbs of healing, trees of the forest, ether and
the Self in all ; these three concerning this outer creation. Then
concerning the Self.   The main breath, the middle breath, the
nether breath, the upper breath and the breath pervasor ; eye,
ear, mind, speech and the skin ; hide, flesh, muscle, bone and
marrow.   Thus the Rishi divided them and said, ' In sets of
five is this universe ; five and five with five and five he relates '."
(Taittiriya Up. I. 7)

PERCEPTION RIGHT AND WRONG.   " As water that
rains in the rough and difficult places, runs to many sides on
the mountain tops, so he that sees separate law and action of
the One Spirit, follows in the track of what he sees.
But as pure water that is poured into pure water, even as it
was such it remains, so is it with the soul of the thinker who
knows God." (Katha Up. II. 1. 14, 15)

PERFECT WAY.   Brahman is both Vidya and Avidya, both
Birth and Non-Birth. The realisation of the Self as the unborn

and the poise of the soul beyond the dualities of birth and death in the infinite and transcendent existence are the conditions of a free and divine life in the Becoming. The one is necessary to the other. It is by participation in the pure unity of the Immobile Brahman that the soul is released from its absorption in the stream of the movement. So released it identifies with the Lord to whom becoming and non-becoming are only modes of His existence and is able to enjoy immortality in the manifestation without being caught in the wheel of Nature's delusions. The necessity of birth ceases, its personal object having been fulfilled ; the freedom of becoming remains. For the Divine enjoys equally and simultaneously the freedom of His eternity and the freedom of His becoming.

By dissolution of ego and of the attachment to birth the soul crosses beyond death ; it is liberated from all limitation in the dualities. Having attained this liberation it accepts becoming as a process of Nature subject to the soul and not binding upon it and by this free and divine becoming enjoys Immortality.

PERSONAL AND IMPERSONAL. It is an error to conceive that the Upanishads teach the true existence only of an impersonal and actionless Brahman, an impersonal God without power or qualities. They declare rather an unknowable that manifests itself to us in a double aspect of Personality and Impersonality. When they wish to speak of this Unknowable in the most comprehensive and general way, they use the neuter and call it *tat*, That ; but this neuter does not exclude the aspect of universal and transcendent Personality acting and governing the world (cf. Kena Up., III). Still, when they intend to make prominent the latter idea they more often prefer to use the masculine *saḥ*, He, or else they employ the term Deva, God or the Divine, or Purusha, the conscious Soul, of whom Prakriti or Maya is the executive Puissance, the Shakti.

PLANES — BASIS OF VEDIC AND VEDANTIC ARRANGEMENT. It takes as its basis the three principles of our ordinary being, mind, life and matter, the triune spiritual principle of Sachchidananda and the link principle of *vijñāna*, supermind, the free or spiritual intelligence, and thus arranges all the larger possible poises of our being in a tier of seven planes, — sometimes regarded as five only, because, only the lower five are wholly accessible to us, — through which the developing being can rise to its perfection.

PRAJNA. Brahman manifests in the Universe of Causal Matter (penetrating and surrounding both the subtle and the gross) as the Cause, Self and Inspirer, poetically styled the Wise One.

" When one sleeps 'and yearns not with any desire, nor sees any dream, that is the perfect slumber. He whose place is the perfect slumber, who is become Oneness, who is wisdom gathered into itself, who is made of mere delight, who enjoys delight unrelated, to whom conscious mind is the door, Prajna, the Lord of Wisdom, He is the third. This is the Almighty, this is the Omniscient, this is the inner Soul, this is the Womb of the Universe, this is the Birth and Destruction of creatures." (Mandukya Up. 5-6)

PRAJNĀ. In all things is the stress of the hidden spirit. We see it as *prajnā*, the *Universal Intelligence*, conscious in things unconscious, active in things inert. The energy of Prajna is what they call Nature. The tree does not and cannot shape itself, the stress of the hidden Intelligence shapes it. He is in the seed of man and in that little particle of matter carries habit, character, types of emotion into the unborn child. Therefore heredity is true ; but if Prajna were not concealed in the seed, heredity would be false, inexplicable, impossible. We see the same stress in the mind, heart, body of man. Because the hidden spirit urges himself on the body, stamps himself on it, expresses himself in it, the body expresses the individuality of the man, the developing and conscious idea or varying type which is myself. Therefore no two faces, no two expressions, no two thumb-impressions even are entirely alike ; every part of the body in some way or other expresses the man. The stress of the spirit shows itself in the mind and heart ; therefore men, families, nations have individuality, run into particular habits of thought and feeling, therefore also they are both alike and dissimilar. Therefore men act and react, not only physically

but spiritually, intellectually, morally on each other, because
there is one self in all creatures expressing itself in various ideas
and forms variously suitable to the idea. The stress of the
hidden Spirit expresses itself again in events and the majestic
course of the world. This is the Zeitgeist, this is the purpose
that runs through the process of the centuries, the changes of
the suns, this is that which makes evolution possible and provides it with a way, means and a goal. " This is He who from
years sempiternal hath ordered perfectly all things."

This is the teachings of Vedanta as we have it in its oldest
form in the Upanishads.

PRAJNĀNA. Wisdom, teleological will or knowledge with a
purpose.

The consciousness which holds an image of things before it
as an object with which it has to enter into relations and to
possess by apprehension and analytic and synthetic cognition ;
the outgoing of apprehensive consciousness to possess its object
in conscious energy, to know it.

PRAJNĀNAM BRAHMA. " Wisdom is the eye of the world,
Wisdom is the sure foundation, Wisdom is Brahman Eternal."
(Aitareya Up. III. 3)

PRAJNĀNETRAM. Wisdom-guided. " Yet, whatsoever thing
here breathes and all that moves and everything that has wings
and whatsoever moves not ; by Wisdom all these are guided
and have their firm abiding in Wisdom. For Wisdom is the eye
of the world, Wisdom is the sure foundation, Wisdom is
Brahman Eternal." (Aitareya Up. III. 3)

PRAKRITI.   Brahman representing Itself as the Motional,
by its power of active Consciousness (Cit) is Nature, Prakriti.

Prakriti, executive Nature as opposed to Purusha, which is
the Soul governing, taking cognizance of and enjoying the works
of Prakriti.

PRĀNA. The English word life does duty for many very
different shades of meaning ; but the word Prana familiar in

the Upanishad and in the language of Yoga is restricted to the life-force whether viewed in itself or in its functionings. The popular sense of Prana was indeed the breath drawn into and thrown out from the lungs and so, in its most material and common sense, the life or the life-breath ; but this is not the philosophic significance of the word as it is used in the Upanishads. The Prana of the Upanishads is the life-energy itself which was supposed to occupy and act in the body with a fivefold movement, each with its characteristic name and each quite as necessary to the functioning of the life of the body as the act of respiration. Respiration in fact is only one action of the chief movement of the life-energy, the first of the five, — the action which is most normally necessary and vital to the maintenance and distribution of the energy in the physical frame, but which can yet be suspended without the life being necessarily destroyed.

The existence of a vital force or life-energy has been doubted by western Science, because that Science concerns itself only with the most external operations of Nature and has as yet no true knowledge of anything except the physical and outward. This Prana, this life-force is not physical in itself ; it is not material energy, but rather a different principle supporting Matter and involved in it. It supports and occupies all forms and without it no physical form could have come into being or could remain in being. It acts in all material forces such as electricity and is nearest to self-manifestation in those that are nearest to pure force ; no material force could exist or act without it, for from it they derive their energy and movement and they are its vehicles. But all material aspects are only field and form of the Prana which is in itself a pure energy, their cause and not their result. It cannot therefore be detected by any physical analysis ; physical analysis can only resolve for us the combinations of those material happenings which are its results and the external signs and symbols of its presence and operation.

While the mind is that movement of Nature in us which represents in the mould of our material and phenomenal existence and within the triple term of the Ignorance the knowledge aspect of the Brahman, the consciousness of the

knower, and body is that which similarly represents the being
of the existent in the mask of phenomenally divisible substance,
so Prana or life-energy represents in the flux of phenomenal
things the force, the active dynamis of the Lord who controls
and enjoys the manifestation of His own being. It is a
universal energy present in every atom and particle of the universe,
and active in every stirring and current of the constant flux and
interchange which constitutes the world.

"Of the Spirit is this breath of Life born : even as shadow
is cast by a man, so is this Life extended in the Spirit and by
the action of the Mind it enters into this body." (Prashna Up.
III. 3)

" I dividing myself into this fivefold support this harp of
God, I am its preserver.' As the spokes meet in the nave of a
wheel, so are all things in the Breath established, the Rigveda
and the Yajur and the Sama, and Sacrifice and Brahminhood
and Kshatriyahood. For all this Universe, yea, all that is
established in the heavens to the Breath is subject : guard us
as a mother watches over little children : give us fortune and
beauty, give us Wisdom." (Prashna Up. II. 3, 6, 13)

" All this universe of motion moves in the Prana and from
the Prana also it proceeded : a mighty terror is He, yea, a
thunderbolt uplifted. Who know Him, are the immortals.

For fear of Him the Fire burns : for fear of Him the Sun
gives heat : for fear of Him Indra and Vayu and Death hasten
in their courses." (Katha Up. II. 3. 2-3)

PRANA AND BODY. " Verily, Prana also is food, and the
body is the eater. The body is established upon Prana and
Prana is established upon the body." (Taittiriya Up. III. 7)

PRANA AND MIND. The proper function of the thought-
mind is to observe, understand, judge with a dispassionate
delight in knowledge and open itself to messages and illuminations playing upon all that it observes and upon all that is
yet hidden from it but must progressively be revealed,
messages and illuminations that secretly flash down to us from
the divine Oracle concealed in light above our mentality
whether they seem to descend through the intuitive mind or

arise from the seeing heart. But this it cannot do rightly because it is pinned to the limitations of the life-energy in the senses, to the discords of sensation and emotion, and to its own limitations of intellectual preference, inertia, straining, self-will which are the forms taken in it by the interference of this desire mind, this psychic Prana. As is said in the Upanishads, our whole mind-consciousness is shot through with the threads and currents of this Prana, this Life-energy that strives and limits, grasps and misses, desires and suffers, and only by its purification can we know and possess our real and eternal self.

PRĀNAMAYA ĀTMA. " There is a second and inner Self which is other than this that is of the substance of food ; and it is made of the vital stuff called Prana. And the Self of Prana fills the Self of food. Now the Self of Prana is made in the image of a man ; according as is the human image of the other, so is it in the image of the man. The main Breath is the head of him, the breath pervasor is his right side and the lower breath is his left side ; ether is his spirit which is the self of him, earth is his lower member whereon he rests abidingly." (Taittiriya Up. II. 2)

" The Gods live and breathe under the dominion of Prana and men and all these that are beasts ; for Prana is the life of created things and therefore they name it the Life-Stuff of the All. Verily, they who worship the Eternal as Prana, reach Life to the uttermost ; for Prana is the life of created things and therefore they name it the Life-Stuff of the All. And this Self of Prana is the soul in the body of the former one which was of food." (Taittiriya Up. II. 3)

PRANAMAYA PURUSA. The Spirit can be poised in the principle of Life, not in Matter. The Spirit so founded becomes the vital self of a vital world, the Life-Soul of a Life-energy in the reign of a consciously dynamic Nature. Absorbed in the experiences of the power and play of a conscious Life, it is dominated by the desire, activity and passion of the rajasic principle proper to vital existence. In the individual this spirit becomes a vital soul *prānamaya puruṣa,* in whose nature the

7

life-energies tyrannise over the mental and physical principles. The physical element in a vital world readily shapes its activities and formations in response to desire and its imaginations, it serves and obeys the passion and power of life and their formations and does not thwart or limit them as it does here on earth where life is a precarious incident in an inanimate Matter. The mental element too is moulded and limited by the life-power, obeys it and helps only to enrich and fulfil the urge of its desires and the energy of its impulses. This vital soul lives in a vital body composed of a substance much subtler than physical matter, it is a substance surcharged with conscious energy, capable of much more powerful perceptions, capacities, sense-activities than any that the gross atomic elements of earth-matter can offer. Man, too, has in himself behind his physical being, subliminal to it, unseen and unknown but very close to it and forming with it the most naturally active part of his existence, this vital soul, this vital nature and this vital body ; a whole vital plane connected with the life-world or desire-world is hidden in us, a secret consciousness in which life and desire find their untrammelled play and their easy self-expression and from there throw their influences and formations on our outer life.

PRĀNA-ŚARĪRA NETA. " A mental being, leader of the life and the body, has set a heart in matter, in matter he has taken his firm foundation. By its knowing the wise see everywhere around them That which shines in its effulgence, a shape of Bliss and immortal." (Mundaka Up. II. 2.8)

PRĀNOBRAHMA. " He knew Prana for the Eternal. For from Prana alone, it appears, are these creatures born and being born they live by Prana and to Prana they go hence and return." (Taittiriya Up. III. 3)

PRAYER FOR FITNESS. " The bull of the hymns of Veda whose visible form is all this Universe, he above the Vedas who sprang from that which is deathless, may Indra increase unto me intellect for my strengthening. O God, may I become a vessel of immortality. May my body be swift to all works, may my tongue drop pure honey. May I hear vast and manifold lore with my ears. O Indra, thou art the sheath of the Eternal and the veil that the workings of brain have drawn over Him ; preserve whole unto me the sacred lore that I have studied." (Taittiriya Up. I. 4)

PREYAS AND *SREYAS*.   The pleasant is not always the right thing, the object to be preferred and selected, nor the unpleasant the wrong thing, the object to be shunned and rejected ; the pleasant and the good, *preyas* and *sreyas,* have to be distinguished, and right reason has to choose.

" One thing is the good and quite another thing is the pleasant, and both seize upon a man with different meanings. Of these who so takes the good, it is well with him ; he falls from the aim of life who chooses the pleasant.

The good and the pleasant come to a man and the thoughtful mind turns all around them and distinguishes.   The wise chooses out the good from the pleasant but the dull soul chooses the pleasant rather than the getting of his good and its having." (Katha Up. I. 2, 1, 2.)

PRTHIVI.   The earth-principle creating habitations of physical form for the soul.

Matter is here the basis and the apparent beginning ; in the language of the Upanishads, *prthvi,* the Earth-principle, is our foundation.

PSYCHIC BEING.   The psychic being came into Nature from the Self, the Divine, and it can turn back from Nature to the silent Divine through the silence of the Self and a supreme spiritual immobility.   Again, an eternal portion of the Divine, this part is by the law of the Infinite inseparable from its Divine whole, this part is indeed itself that Whole, except in its frontal appearance, its frontal separative self-experience ; it may awaken to that reality and plunge into it to the apparent extinction or at least the merging of the individual existence. A small nucleus here in the mass of our ignorant Nature, so that it is described in the Upanishad as no bigger than a man's thumb, it can by the spiritual influx enlarge itself and embrace the whole world with the heart and mind in an intimate communion or oneness. Or it may become aware of its eternal Companion and elect to live for ever in His presence, in an imperishable union and oneness as the eternal lover with the eternal Beloved, which of all spiritual experiences is the most intense in beauty and rapture.

PURIFICATION. If there is to be an active perfection of our being, the first necessity is a purification of the working of the instruments which it now uses for a music of discords. The being itself, the spirit, the divine Reality in man stands in no need of purification ; it is for ever pure, not affected by the faults of its instrumentation or the stumblings of mind and heart and body in their work, as the sun, says the Upanishad, is not touched or stained by the faults of the eye of vision. Mind, heart, the soul of vital desire, the life in the body are the seats of impurity ; it is they that must be set right if the working of the spirit is to be a perfect working and not marked by its present greater or less concession to the devious pleasure of the lower nature.

"Eye cannot seize, speech cannot grasp Him, nor these other godheads ; not by austerity can he be held nor by works ; only when the inner being is purified by a glad serenity of knowledge, then indeed, meditating, one beholds the Spirit indivisible. This self is subtle and has to be known by a thought-mind into which the life-force has made its fivefold entry ; all the conscious heart of creatures is shot through and inwoven with the currents of the life-force and only when it is purified can this Self manifest its power. Whatever world the man whose inner being is purified sheds the light of his mind upon, and whatsoever desires he cherishes, that world he takes by conquest, and those desires. Then, let whosoever seeks for success and well-being approach with homage a self-knower." (Mundaka Up. III. 1. 8-10)

PURUṢA. Brahman representing Itself in the universe as the Stable, by Its immutable existence (Sat), is Purusha, God, Spirit.

In the oceanic stir and change of universal Nature the soul or *purusa* is the standing-point, stable, unmoving, unchanging, eternal — *nityaḥ sarvagatah sthānur acaloyam sanātanaḥ.* In the whole the Purusha or soul is one, — there is One Spirit which supports the stir of the Universe, not many. In the individual the One Purusha has three stages of personality ; He is One, but triple *tryṛt.* The Upanishads speak of *two birds on one tree,* of which one eats the fruit of the tree, the other, seated on a higher branch, does not eat but watches its fellow ; one is *īśa* or Lord of itself, the other is *anīśa,* not lord of itself, and it is when the eater looks up and perceives the greatness of the watcher and fills himself with it that grief, death, subjection — in one word *māyā,* ignorance and illusion, cease to touch him. There are two unborn who are male and one unborn who is female ; she is the tree with its sweet and bitter fruit, the two are the birds. One of the unborn enjoys her sweetness, the other has put it away from him. These are the two Purushas, the *aksara* or immutable spirit, and *ksara* or apparently mutable, and the tree or woman is Prakriti, universal Energy, Nature. The *kṣara* Purusha is the soul in Nature and enjoying Nature, the *akṣara.* Purusha is the soul above Nature and watching her. But there is One who is not seated on the tree but occupies and possesses it, who is not only lord of Himself, but lord of all that is ; He is higher than the *kṣara,* higher than the *akṣara,* He is Purushottama, the Soul one with God, with the all.

Vide Dvā suparṇā.

" The mind is higher than the senses, and higher than the mind is the genius, above the genius is she Mighty Spirit, and higher than the Mighty One is the Unmanifested.

But highest above the Unmanifested is the Purusha who pervades all and alone he has no sign nor feature. Mortal man knowing Him is released into immortality." (Katha Up. II. 3. 7-8)

" The Purusha is all this that is, what has been and what is yet to be ; he is the master of Immortality and he is whatever grows by food." (Shvetashvatara Up. III. 15)

QUALITIED *vs.* QUALITYLESS. Indian philosophy has drawn distinction between the Qualitied and the Qualityless Brahman. The Upanishad indicates clearly enough the relative nature of this opposition, when it speaks of the Supreme as the " Qualitied who is without qualities " (*nirguṇo guṇī*).

The whole action of the universe may be regarded from a certain point of view as the expression and shaping out in various ways of the numberless and infinite qualities of the Brahman. His being assumes by conscious Will all kinds of properties, shapings of the stuff of conscious being, habits as it were of cosmic character and power of dynamic self-consciousness, *guṇas*, into which all the cosmic action can be resolved. But by none of these nor by all of them nor by their utmost infinite potentiality is He bound ; He is above all His qualities and on a certain plane of being rests free from them. The Nirguna or Unqualitied is not incapable of qualities, rather it is this very Nirguna or No-Quality who manifests Himself as Saguna, as *anantaguṇa*, infinite quality, since He contains all in His absolute capacity of boundlessly varied self-revelation. He is free from them in the sense of exceeding them ; and indeed if He were not free from them they could not be infinite ; God would be subject to His qualities, bound by His nature, Prakriti would be supreme and Purusha its creation and plaything. The Eternal is bound neither by quality nor absence of quality, neither by Personality nor by Impersonality ; He is Himself, beyond all our positive and all our negative definitions.

RASA. " Verily, it is no other than the delight behind existence. When he has got him this delight, then it is that this creation becomes a thing of bliss." (Taittiriya Up. II. 7)

REALISATION. " Realising the God by attainment to Him through spiritual Yoga, even the Ancient of Days who hath entered deep into that which is hidden and is hard to see, for he is established in our secret being and lodged in the cavern heart of things, the wise and steadfast man casts away from him joy and sorrow." (Katha Up. I. 2. 12)

REBIRTH. There are numerous important passages in almost all the Upanishads positively affirming rebirth, and, in any case, the Upanishads admit the survival of the personality after death and its passage into other worlds. If there is survival in other worlds and also a final destiny of liberation into Brahman for souls embodied here, rebirth imposes itself.

REMORSE AND TORMENT. " Who knows the Bliss of the Eternal He fears not for aught in this world or elsewhere. Verily, to him comes not remorse and her torment saying ' Why have I left undone the good and have I done that which was evil ? ' For he who knows the Eternal, knows these and delivers from them his Spirit ; yea, he knows both evil and good for what they are and delivers his Spirit, who knows the Eternal." (Taittiriya Up. II. 9)

RENUNCIATION. We must be prepared to leave behind on the path not only that which we stigmatise as evil, but that which seems to us to be good, yet is not the one good. There are things which were beneficial, helpful, which seemed perhaps at one time the one thing desirable, and yet once their work is done, once they are attained, they become obstacles and even hostile forces when we are called to advance beyond them. There are desirable states of the soul which it is dangerous to rest in after they have been mastered, because then we do not march on to the wider kingdoms of God beyond. Even divine realisations must not be clung to, if they are not the divine realisation in its utter essentiality and completeness. We must rest at nothing less than the All, nothing short of the utter transcendence. And if we can thus be free in the spirit, we shall find out all the wonder of God's workings ; we shall find that in inwardly renouncing everything we have lost nothing. " By all this abandoned thou shalt come to enjoy the All." For everything is kept for us and restored to us but with a wonderful change and transfiguration into the All-Good and the All-Beautiful, the All-Light and the All-Delight of Him who is for ever pure and infinite and the mystery and the miracle that ceases not through the ages.

The egoistic possession, the making of things our own in the sense of the ego's claim on God and beings and the world, *parigraha*, must be renounced in order that this greater thing, this large, universal and perfect life, may come. *Tyaktena bhunjīthāḥ,* by renouncing the egoistic sense of desire and possession, the soul enjoys divinely its self and the universe.

The renunciation intended is an absolute renunciation of the principle of desire founded on the principle of egoism and not a renunciation of world-existence.

RESTING PLACE.   " As birds wing towards their resting tree, so do all these depart into the Supreme Spirit." (Prashna Up. IV. 7)

RESTRAINT.   " Let the wise man restrain speech in his mind and mind in the Self, and knowledge in the Great-Self, and that again let him restrain in the Self that is at peace." (Katha Up. I. 3. 13)

SACCIDĀNANDA.   The pure state of Atman ; it may either remain self-contained as if apart from the universe or overlook, embrace and possess it as the Lord. In fact it does both simultaneously.

The self-manifestation of a supreme Unknowable, Para-Brahman or Para-Purusha.

SAKTI.   The self-existent, self-cognitive, self-effective Power of the Lord (Ishvara) which expresses itself in the workings of Prakriti.

" They beheld the self-force of the Divine Being deep hidden by its own conscious modes of working." (Shvetashvatara Up. I. 3)

SACRIFICE.   The whole process of the universe is in its very nature a sacrifice, voluntary or involuntary. Self-fulfil-ment by self-immolation, to grow by giving is the universal law. That which refuses to give itself, is still the food of the cosmic Powers. " The eater eating is eaten " is the formula, pregnant and · terrible, in which the Upanishad sums up this aspect of the universe, and in another passage men are described as the cattle of the gods. It is only when the law is recognised and voluntarily accepted that this kingdom of death can be overpassed and by the works of sacrifice Immortality made possible and attained.

SAMHITĀ. Combination. " Five Great *samhitās* ; Concerning the Words ; Concerning the Shining Fires ; Concerning the Knowledge ; Concerning Progeny ; Concerning Self. These are called the great Samhitas.

Now concerning the Worlds. Earth is the first form, the heavens are the second form ; ether is the linking ; air is the joint of the linking. Thus far concerning the Worlds.

Next concerning the Shining Fires. Fire is the first form, the Sun is the latter form ; the waters are the linking ; electricity is the joint of linking. Thus far concerning the Shining Fires.

Next concerning the Knowledge. The Master is the first form, the disciple is the latter form. Knowledge is the linking. Exposition is the joint of the linking. Thus far concerning the Knowledge.

Next concerning Progeny. The mother is the first form ; the father is the latter form, Progeny is the linking, act of procreation is the joint of linking. Thus far concerning Progeny.

Next concerning Self. The upper jaw is the first form ; the lower jaw is the latter form ; speech is the linking ; the tongue is the joint of linking. Thus far concerning Self." (Taittiriya Up. I. 3)

SANJNĀNA. Awareness by contact.

The contact of consciousness with an image of things by which there is a sensible possession of it in substance ; the inbringing movement of apprehensive consciousness which draws the object placed before it back to itself so as to possess it in conscious substance, to feel it.

The state described by the Upanishad in which one sees, hears, feels, touches, senses in every way the Brahman and the Brahman only, for all things have become to the consciousness only that and have no other, separate or independent existence, is not a mere figure of speech, but the exact description of the fundamental action of the pure sense, the spiritual object of the pure *sanjnāna.*

ŚANTI PĀTHA. Peace chant. Hari Om! Be peace to us Mitra. Be peace to us Varuna. Be peace to us Aryaman. Be peace to us Indra and Brihaspati. May farstriding Vishnu be peace to us. Adoration to the Eternal. Adoration to thee, O Vayu. Thou, thou are the visible Eternal and as the visible eternal I will declare thee. I will declare Righteousness! I will declare Truth! May that protect me! May that protect the speaker! Yea, may it protect me! May it protect the speaker, Om! Peace! Peace! Peace!

Hari Om! Together may He protect us, together may He possess us, together may we make unto us force and virility. May our reading be full of light and power. May we never hate. Om! Peace! Peace! Peace!

Om! " I am He that moves the Tree of the Universe and my glory is like the shoulders of a high-mountain. I am lofty and pure like sweet nectar in the strong, I am the shining riches of the world, I am the deep thinker, the deathless One who decays not from the beginning."

This is Trishanku's voicing of the Veda and the hymn of his self-knowledge. Om! Peace! Peace! Peace!

SAT.   Essence of our being, pure infinite and undivided, as opposed to this divisible being which founds itself on the constant changeableness of physical substance. Sat is the divine counterpart of physical substance.

SAT AND *ASAT.*   " One becomes as the unexisting, if he knows the Eternal as negation ; but if one knows of the Eternal that He is, then men know him for the saint and the one reality." (Taittiriya Up. II. 6)

SATYAMEVA JAYATE.   " It is Truth that conquers and not falsehood ; by Truth was stretched out the path of the journey of the gods, by which the sages winning their desire ascend there where Truth has its Supreme abode." (Mundaka Up. III. 1. 6)

SELF. The entity which represents the Brahman in the cosmos, the self of the living and thinking creature, man. This self is not an external mask; it is not form of the mind or form of the life or form of the body. It is something that supports these and makes them possible, something that can say positively like the gods, " I am " and not only " I seem ".

" He is the secret Self in all existences and does not manifest Himself to the vision : yet is He seen by the seers of the subtle by a subtle and perfect understanding." (Katha Up. I. 3. 12)

Self-Fourfold : The Self that becomes all these forms of things is the Virat or universal Soul ; the Self that creates all these forms is Hiranyagarbha, the luminous or creatively perceptive Soul ; the Self that contains all these things involved in it is Prajna, the conscious Cause or originally determining Soul ; beyond all these is the Absolute who permits all this unreality, but has no dealings with it.

Self of Knowledge : " This Self is a self of Knowledge, an inner light in the heart ; he is conscious being common to all the states of being and moves in both worlds. He becomes a dream-self and passes beyond this world and its forms of death. There are two planes of this conscious being, this and the other worlds ; a third state is their place of joining, the state of dream, and when he stands in this place of their joining, he sees both planes of his existence, this world and the other world. When he sleeps, he takes the substance of this world in which all is and himself undoes and himself builds by his own illumination, his own light ; when this conscious being sleeps, he becomes luminous with his self-light. . . . There are no roads nor chariots, nor joys nor pleasures, nor tanks nor ponds nor rivers, but he creates them by his own light, for he is the maker. By sleep he casts off his body and unsleeping sees those that sleep ; he preserves by his life-breath this lower nest and goes forth, immortal, from his nest ; immortal, he goes where he wills, the *Golden Purusha*, the solitary Swan. They say, ' the country of waking only is his, for the things which he sees when awake, these only he sees when asleep '; but there he is his own self-light." (Brihadaranyaka Up. IV. 3. 7, 9-12, 14)

Self and Learning : " This Self is not won by exegesis, nor by brainpower, nor by much learning of Scripture." (Mundaka Up. III. 2. 3)

Self and Tapasyā : " This is the life in things that shines manifested by all these beings ; a man of knowledge coming wholly to know this, draws back from creeds and too much disputings. In the Self his delight, at play in the Self, doing works, — the best is he among the knowers of the Eternal." (Mundaka Up. III. 1. 4)

Self and Weakness : Man is given faith in himself, his ideas and his powers that he may work and create and rise to greater things and in the end bring his strength as a worthy offering to the altar of the Spirit. This spirit, says the Scripture, is not to be won by the weak, *nāyam ātmā balahinena labhyaḥ.* All paralysing self-distrust has to be discouraged, all doubt of our strength to accomplish, for that is a false assent to impotence, an imagination of weakness and a denial of the omnipotence of the spirit. A present incapacity, however heavy may seem its pressure, is only a trial of faith and a temporary difficulty.

" This Self cannot be won by any who is without strength, nor with error in the seeking, nor by an askesis without the true mark : but when a man of knowledge strives by these means his Self enters into Brahman, his abiding place." (Mundaka Up. III. 2. 4)

SELF-DEVELOPMENT. Man can evolve himself from plane to plane of his own being and embrace on each successively his oneness with the world and with Sachchidananda realised as the Purusha and Prakriti, Conscious-Soul and Nature-Soul of that plane, taking into himself the action of the lower grades of being as he ascends. He may, that is to say, work out by a sort of inclusive process of self-enlargement and transformation the evolution of the material into the divine or spiritual man. This seems to have been the method of the most ancient sages of which we get some glimpse in the Rig Veda and some of the Upanishads.

SELF-KNOWLEDGE. Self-knowledge of all kinds is on the straight path to the knowledge of the real Self. The Upanishad tells us that the Self-existence has so set the doors of the soul that they turn outwards and most men look outward into the appearances of things ; only the rare soul that is ripe for a calm thought and steady wisdom turns its eye inward, sees the Self and attains to immortality. To this turning of the eye inward psychological self-observation and analysis is a great and effective introduction.

Self-knowledge comes by an inner meditation through which the eternal self becomes apparent to us in our own self-existence.

SENSES. "He that is without knowledge with his mind ever unapplied, the senses are to him as wild horses and will not obey their driver. But he that has knowledge with his mind ever applied his senses are to him as noble steeds and they obey the driver." (Katha Up. I. 3. 5, 6)
"The calm soul having comprehended the separateness of the senses and the rising of them and their setting and their separate emergence, puts from him pain and sorrow." (Katha Up. II. 3. 6)

SEPARATION OF PURUSHA. "The Purusha, the Spirit within, who is no larger than the finger of a man is seated for ever in the heart of creatures : one must separate Him with patience from one's own body as one separates from a blade of grass its main fibre. Thou shalt know Him for the Bright Immortal, yea, for the Bright Immortal." (Katha Up. II. 3. 17)

SEVEN STEPS. "Seven steps has the ground of the Ignorance, seven steps has the ground of the knowledge." (Mahopanishad. V. 1)

SEVEN TONGUES. "Kali, the black, Karali, the terrible, Manojava, thought-swift, Sulohita, blood-red, Sudhumravarna, smoke-hued, Sphulingi, scattering sparks, Vishvaruchi, the all-beautiful, these are the seven swaying tongues of the fire." (Mundaka Up. I. 2. 4)

SEVEN WORLDS. When *tapas* or energy of self-conscience dwells upon *sat* or pure existence as its basis, the result is *satyaloka* or world of true existence.

When *tapas* dwells upon active power of *cit* as its basis, the result is *tapoloka* or world of energy of self-conscience.

When *tapas* dwells upon active Delight of being as its basis, the result is *Janaloka*, world of creative Delight.

(These three worlds of the Spirit constitute the *parārdha*.)

In the lower creation, *aparārdha*, also there are three principles, Matter, Life and Mind.

In the organisation of consciousness to which we belong, *tapas* dwells upon Matter as its basis. This is *Bhūrloka*, the material world, the world of formal becoming.

The organisation of consciousness in which dynamic Life-force is the basis, is *bhuvarloka*, the world of free vital becoming in form.

The organised state of consciousness in which Mind determines its own forms is *svarloka*, world of free, pure and luminous mentality.

Between these two creations, linking them together, is the world of organisation of consciousness of which the Infinite Truth of things is the foundation. This world is *maharloka*, world of large consciousness.

" Seven are these worlds in which move the life-forces that are hidden within the secret heart as their dwelling-place seven and seven." (Mundaka Up. II. 1. 8)

ŚIKṢĀ. Science of Phonetics. " The elements : Syllable and Accent, Pitch and Effort, Even Tone and Continuity." (Taittiriya Up. I. 2)

SIN. Sin, in the conception of the Veda, is that which excites and hurries the faculties into deviation from the good path. There is a straight road or road of naturally increasing light and truth leading over infinite levels and towards infinite vistas by which the law of our nature should normally take us towards our fulfilment. Sin compels it instead to travel with stumblings amid uneven and limited tracts and along crooked windings.

From Sin to Felicity : " O god Agni, knowing all things that are manifested, lead us by the good path to the felicity ; remove from us the devious attractions of sin." (Isha Up. 18)

SOUL. " Smaller than the hundredth part of the tip of a hair, the soul of the living being is capable of infinity. Male is he not nor female nor neuter, but is joined to whatever body he takes as his own." (Shvetashvatara Up. V. 9, 10)

SOUL AND MANIFESTATION. The Upanishad admits three states of the soul in relation to the manifested universe : terrestrial life by birth in the body, the survival of the individual soul after death in other states and the immortal existence which being beyond birth and death, beyond manifestation can yet enter into forms as the Inhabitant and embrace Nature as its lord.

SOUL AND NATURE. The Soul and Nature are only two aspects of the eternal Brahman, an apparent duality which founds the operations of his universal existence. The Soul is without origin and eternal ; Nature too is without origin and eternal ; but the modes of Nature and the lower forms she assumes to our conscious experience have an origin in the transactions of these two entities.

SOUL'S ASCENSION. The soul that aspires to perfection, draws back and upward, says the Upanishad, from the physical into the vital and from the vital into the mental Purusha, — from the mental into the knowledge-soul and from that self of knowledge into the bliss Purusha. This self of bliss is the conscious foundation of perfect Sachchidananda and to pass into it completes the soul's ascension.

SPEECH. " Speech is the essence of man." (Chhandogya Up. I. 1. 2)

SPIRITUAL KNOWLEDGE. The spiritual knowledge may be awakened by the urging of the spirit within us, its call to this or that Yoga, this or that way of oneness. Or it may come to us by hearing of the truth from others and the moulding of the mind into the sense of that to which it listens with faith and concentration. But however arrived at, it carries us beyond death to immortality.

STHĀNU. As we are subordinate and an aspect of an infinite Movement, so the movement is subordinate and an aspect of something other than itself, of a great timeless, spaceless Stability, *sthānu,* which is immutable, inexhaustible and unexpended, not acting though containing all this action, not energy, but pure existence.

STYLE OF THE UPANISHADS. The Upanishads, being vehicles of illumination and not of instruction, composed for seekers who had already a general familiarity with the ideas of the Vedic and Vedantic seers and even some personal experience of the truths on which they were founded, dispense in their style with expressed transitions of thought and the development of implied or subordinate notions.

SUBLIMINAL. Our waking state is unaware of its connection with the subliminal being, although it receives from it — but without any knowledge of the place of origin — the inspirations, intuitions, ideas, will-suggestions, sense-suggestions, urges to action that rise from below or from behind our limited surface existence. Sleep, like trance, opens the gate of the subliminal to us; for in sleep, as in trance, we retire behind the veil of the limited waking personality and it is behind this veil that the subliminal has its existence. But we receive the records of our sleep experience through dream and in dream figures and not in that condition which might be called an inner waking and which is the most accessible form of the trance state, nor through the supernormal clarities of vision and other more luminous and concrete ways of communication developed by the inner subliminal cognition when it gets into habitual or occasional conscious connection with our waking self. The subliminal, with the subconscious as an annex of itself, — for the subconscious is also a part of the behind-the-veil entity, — is the seer of inner things and of supraphysical experiences; the surface subconscious is only a transcriber. It is for this reason that the Upanishad describes the subliminal being as the Dream Self because it is normally in dreams, visions, absorbed states of inner experience that we enter into and are part of its experiences, — just as it describes the superconscient as the Sleep Self because normally all mental or sensory experiences cease when we enter this super-conscience. For in the deeper trance into which the touch of the superconscient plunges our mentality, no record from it or tran-script of its contents can normally reach us ; it is only by an especial or an unusual development, in a supernormal condition or through a break or rift in our confined normality, that we can be on the surface conscious of the contacts or messages of the Superconscience. But, in spite of these figurative names of dream-state and sleep-state, the field of both these states of conscious-ness was clearly regarded as a field of reality not less than that of the waking state in which our movements of perceptive con-sciousness are a record of transcript of physical things and of our contacts with the physical universe.

SUN. In the Upanishad the sun is the symbol of the supra-mental Truth and it is said that those who pass into it may return but those who pass through the gates of the sun itself do not ; possibly this means that an ascent into the Supermind itself above the golden lid of Overmind was the definitive liberation. The Veda speaks of the Truth hidden by a Truth where the Sun looses his horses from his car and there all the myriad rays are drawn together into one and that was considered the goal. The Isha Upanishad also speaks of the golden lid hiding the face of the Truth by removing which the Law of the Truth is seen, and the highest knowledge in which the one Purusha is known (*so'hamasmi*) is described as the *kalyāṇatma* form of the Sun. All this seems to refer to the supramental states of which the Sun is the symbol.

In the inner sense of the Veda, Surya, the Sun-God, represents the divine Illumination of the Kavi which exceeds mind and forms the pure self-luminous Truth of things. His principal power is self revelatory knowledge, termed in the Veda " Sight ". His realm is described as the Truth, the Law, the Vast. He is the Fosterer or Increaser, for he enlarges and opens man's dark and limited being into a luminous and infinite consciousness. He is the sole Seer of Oneness and Knower of the Self, and leads him to the highest Sight. He is Yama, Controller or Ordainer, for he governs man's action and manifested being by the direct Law of the Truth, *satyadharma,* and therefore by the

8

right principle of our nature, *yāthātathyataḥ* a luminous power
proceeding from the Father of all existence, he reveals in himself the divine Purusha of whom all beings are the manifestations.
His rays are the thoughts that proceed luminously from the Truth,
the Vast, but become deflected and distorted, broken up and
disordered in the reflecting and dividing principle, Mind. They
form there the golden lid which covers the face of the Truth.
The Seer prays (Isha Up. 15-16) to Surya to cast them into right
order and relation and then draw them together into the unity
of revealed truth. The result of this inner process is the perception of the oneness of all beings in the divine Soul of the
Universe.

Fire-Sun. "Fire is this burning and radiant Sun, he is the
One lustre and all-knowing Light, he is the highest heaven of
spirits. With a thousand rays he burns and exists in a hundred
existences ; lo this Sun that rises, he is the Life of all his creatures." (Prashna Up. 1. 8)

SUPREME. "This that is awake in those who sleep creating
desire upon desire, this Purusha, Him they call the Bright One,
Him Brahman, Him Immortality, and in Him are all the worlds
established : none goes beyond Him. *This is That thou seekest."*
(Katha Up. II, 2. 8)

"He, the divine, the formless Spirit, even he is outward and
the inward and he the Unborn ; he is beyond life, beyond mind,
luminous, Supreme beyond the immutable. Life and mind and the
senses are born from him and the sky, and the wind, and light,
and the waters and earth upholding all that is. Fire is the head
of Him and his eyes are the Sun and the Moon, the quarters his
organs of hearing and the revealed Vedas are his voice, air is his
breath, the universe is his heart, Earth lies at his feet. He is
the inner Self in all beings.

From Him is fire, of which the Sun is the fuel, then rain from
the Soma, herbs upon the earth, and the male casts his seed
into woman : thus are these many peoples born from the Spirit.
From him are the hymns of the Rig Veda, the Sama and the
Yajur, initiation, and all sacrifices and works of sacrifice, and
dues given, the year and the giver of the sacrifice and the worlds,
on which the moon shines and the sun.

And from Him have issued many gods, and demi-gods and men and beasts and birds, the main breath and downward breath, and rice and barley, and askesis and faith and Truth, and chastity and rule of right practice. The seven breaths are born from Him and the seven lights and kinds of fuel and the seven oblations and these seven worlds in which move the life-breaths set within with the secret heart for their dwelling-place, seven and seven.

From Him are the oceans and all these mountains and from Him flow rivers of all forms, and from Him are all plants, and sensible delight which makes the soul abide with the material elements. The Spirit is all this universe ; he is works and askesis and the Brahman, supreme and immortal. O fair son, he who knows this hidden in the secret heart scatters even here in this world the knot of the Ignorance." (Mundaka Up. II. 1. 2 to 10)

SUPREME SOUL. All relations of Soul and Nature are circumstances in the eternity of Brahman ; sense and quality, their reflectors and constituents, are this supreme Soul's devices for the presentation of the workings that his own energy in things constantly liberates into movement. He is himself beyond the limitations of the senses, sees all things but not with the physical eye, hears all things but not with the physical ear, is aware of all things but not with the limiting mind — mind which represents but cannot truly know. Not determined by any qualities, he possesses and determines in his substance all qualities and enjoys this qualitative action of his own Nature. He is attached to nothing, bound by nothing, fixed to nothing that he does ; calm, he supports in a large and immortal freedom all the action and movement and passion of his universal Shakti. He becomes all that is in the universe ; that which is in us is he and all that we experience outside ourselves is he. The inward and the outward, the far and the near, the moving and the unmoving, all this he is at once. He is the subtlety of the subtle which is beyond our knowledge, even as he is the density of force and substance which offers itself to the grasp of our minds. He is indivisible and the One, but seems to divide himself in forms and creatures and appears as all these separate existences. All things can get back in him, can return in the Spirit to the indivisible unity of their self-existence. All is eternally born from him, upborne in his eternity, taken eternally back into his oneness. He is the light of all lights and luminous beyond all the darkness of our ignorance. He is knowledge and the object of knowledge.

SVARAT. The spirit is in possession of knowledge and will, of which it is the source and cause and not a subject; therefore in proportion as the soul assumes its divine or spiritual being, it assumes also control of the movements of its nature. It becomes, in the ancient language, *svarat,* free and self-ruler over the kingdom of its own life and being.

TAIJASA. " He whose place is the dream, who is wise of the inward, who has seven limbs, to whom there are nineteen doors, who feels and enjoys subtle objects, Taijasa, the Inhabitant in Luminous Mind, He is the second." (Mandukya Up. 4)

TAPAS. Tapas means literally heat, afterwards any kind of energism, askesis, austerity of conscious force acting upon itself or its object. The world was created by Tapas in the form, says the ancient image, of an egg, which being broken, again by Tapas, heat of incubation of conscious force, the Purusha emerged, Soul in Nature, like a bird from the egg. It may be observed that the usual translation of the word *tapasyā* in English books, " penance ", is quite misleading—the idea of penance entered rarely into the austerities practised by Indian ascetic. Nor was mortification of the body the essence even of the most severe and self-afflicting austerities; the aim was rather an overpassing of the hold of the bodily nature on the consciousness or else a supernormal energising of the consciousness and will to gain some spiritual or other object.

The energising conscious-power of cosmic being by which the world is created, maintained and governed; it includes all concepts of force, will, energy, power, everything dynamic and dynamising.

Tapas and Brahman : " By askesis do thou seek to know the

Eternal, for concentration in thought is the Eternal." (Taittiriya Up. III. 4)

" Theirs is the heaven of the Spirit in whom are established askesis and holiness and in whom Truth has her dwelling. Theirs is the heaven of the Spirit, the world all spotless, in whom there is neither crookedness nor lying nor any illusion." (Prashna Up. I. 15-16)

" They who in the forest follow after faith and self-discipline, calm and full of knowledge, living upon alms, cast from them the dust of their passions, and through the gate of the Sun they pass on there where is the Immortal, the Spirit, the Self undecaying and imperishable." (Mundaka Up. I. 2. 11)

TEACHER'S PRAYER. " May the Brahmacharins come unto me. Swaha ! From here and there may the Brahmacharins come unto me. Swaha ! May the Brahmacharins set forth unto me. Swaha ! May the Brahmacharins attain self mastery, Swaha ! May the Brahmacharins attain to peace of soul. Swaha ! May I be a name among the folk ! Swaha ! May I be the first of the wealthy ! Swaha ! O Glorious Lord, into that which is thou may I enter, Swaha ! Do thou also enter into me, O shining One. Swaha! Thou art a river with a hundred branching streams, O Lord of Grace, in thee may I wash me clean. Swaha ! As the waters of a river pour down the steep, as the months of the year hasten to the old age of days, O Lord that cherisheth, so may the Brahmacharins come to me from all the regions. Swaha ! O Lord, thou art my neighbour, thou dwellest very near me. Come to me, be my light and sun." (Taittiriya Up. I. 4)

Teacher and Disciple : " Together may we attain glory, together to the radiance of holiness." (Taittiriya Up. I. 1. 3)

THERE AS HERE. " What is in this world, is also in the other : and what is in the other, that again is in this : who thinks he sees difference here, from death to death he goes." (Katha Up. II. 1. 10)

THOUGHT AND BRAHMAN. " He by whom It is not thought out, has the thought of It ; he by whom It is thought

out, knows It not. It is unknown to the discernment of those
who discern of It, by those who seek not to discern of It, It is
discerned. When it is known by perception that reflects it, then
one has the thought of It." (Kena Up. II. 3. 4)

THREE MANSIONS. "He has three mansions in His city,
three dreams wherein He dwells, and of each in turn He says
'Lo, this is my habitation' and 'This is my habitation' and
'This is my habitation'." (Aitareya Up. I. 3. 12)

THUMB-SIZE PURUSHA. "The Purusha who is seated
in the midst of our self is no larger than the size of a
man's thumb; He is the Lord of what was and what shall
be. Him having seen one shrinks not from aught, nor abhors
any.
    The Purusha that is within us is no larger than the size of a
man's thumb: He is like a blazing fire that is without smoke,
He is lord of His past and His future. He alone is today and
He alone shall be tomorrow." (Katha Up. II. I, 12, 13)

TIME. That mysterious condition of universal mind which
alone makes the ordering of the universe in Space possible,
although its own relations to matter are necessarily determined
by material events and movements — for itself subtle as well
as infinite, it offers no means by which it can be materially
measured.
    kāla :   Time in its essentiality.
    samvatsara :   Time in its periods determined by movement in
Space.
    "Some speak of the self-nature of things, others say that it is
Time." (Shvetashvatara Up. VI. 1)
    "Two are the forms of Brahman, Time and the Timeless."
(Maitri Up. VI. 15)

TRAVELLER. "The Soul of man, a traveller, wanders in
this cycle of Brahman, huge, a totality of lives, a totality of
states, thinking itself different from the Impeller of the
journey. Accepted by Him, it attains its goal of Immortality."
(Shvetashvatara Up. I. 6)

TRISHANKU'S HYMN OF SELF-KNOWLEDGE. " I am He that moves the Tree of the Universe and my glory is like the shoulders of high-mountain, I am lofty and pure like sweet nectar in the strong, I am the shining riches of the world, I am the deep thinker, the deathless One who decays not from the beginning." (Taittiriya Up. I. 10)

TURĪYA. " He who is neither inward-wise, nor outward-wise, nor both inward and outward wise, nor wisdom self-gathered, nor possessed of wisdom, nor unpossessed of wisdom, He Who is unseen and incommunicable, unseizable, featureless, unthinkable, and unnameable, Whose essentiality is awareness of the Self in its single existence, in Whom all phenomena dissolve, Who is Calm, Who is Good, Who is the One than whom there is no other, Him they deem the fourth : He is the Self, He is the object of Knowledge." (Mandukya Up. 7)

TWO BIRDS. The Self outside nature does not become ; it is immutable as well as eternal. The Self in Nature becomes, it changes its states and forms. Because of these two positions of the Self, in Nature and out of Nature, moving in the movement and seated above the movement, active in the development and eating the fruits of the tree of Life or inactive and simply regarding, there are two possible states of conscious existence directly opposed to each other of which the human soul is capable.
Vide Dual Status of the Soul ; *dvā suparṇā ;* Purusha.

UDGITHA. Ascension as well as circling upward of the voice or the soul in song. When the Vedic singer said *udgāyām,* the physical idea was that, perhaps, of the song rising upwards, but he had also the psychical idea of the soul rising up in song to the gods and fulfilling by its meeting with them and entering into them its expressed aspiration.

UMA. Uma is the supreme Nature from whom the whole cosmic action takes its birth ; she is the pure summit and the highest power of the One who here shines out in many forms.

From this supreme Nature which is also the supreme Consciousness the gods must learn their own truth ; they must proceed by reflecting it in themselves instead of limiting themselves to their own lower movement. For she has the knowledge and consciousness of the One, while the lower nature of mind, life and body can only envisage the many.

UNIVERSAL BEING. A spirit who immeasurably fills and surrounds all this movement with himself — for indeed the movement too is himself — and who throws on all that is finite the splendour of his garment of infinity, a bodiless and million-bodied spirit whose hands of strength and feet of swiftness are on every side of us, whose heads and eyes and faces are those innumerable visages which we see wherever we turn, whose ear is everywhere listening to the silence of eternity and the music of the worlds is the universal Being in whose embrace we live.

UNIVERSE. To the Vedantic thinkers the universe, the manifest Brahman, was a harmony of worlds within worlds ; they beheld a space within our space but linked with it, they were aware of a time connected with our time but different from it. This earth was *bhūr*. Rising in soul into the air above the earth, the *antariksam*, they thought they came into contact with other sevenfold earths in which just as here matter is the predominant principle, so there nervous or vital energy is the main principle, or else *manas,* still dependent upon matter and vital energy ; these earths they called *bhuvar.* And rising beyond this atmosphere into the etherial void they believed themselves to be aware of other worlds which they called *svar* or heaven, where again, in its turn, mind, free, blithe, delivered from its struggle to impose itself in a world not its own upon matter and nerve-life, is the medium of existence and the governing Force.

"All this is for habitation by the Lord." (Isha Up. I)

Universe — course and movement : An infinite, indivisible existence all-blissful in its pure self-consciousness moves out of its fundamental purity into the varied play of Force that is consciousness, into the movement of Prakriti which is the play of Maya. The delight of its existence is at first self-gathered, absorbed, subconscious in the basis of the physical universe ; then emergent in a great mass of neutral movement which is not yet what we call sensation ; then further emergent with the growth of mind and ego in the triple vibration of pain, pleasure and indifference originating from the limitation of the force of consciousness in the form and from its exposure to shocks of the universal Force which it finds alien to it and out of harmony with its own measure and standard ; finally, the conscious emergence of the full Sachchidananda in its creations by universality, by‑ equality, by self-possession and conquest of Nature.   This is the course and movement of the world.

UNKNOWABLE.   The Unknowable, if it is at all, may be a supreme state of Sachchidananda beyond our highest conceptions of existence, consciousness and bliss ; that is what was evidently meant by the Asat, the Non-Existent of the Taittiriya Upanishad, which alone was in the beginning and out of which the existent was born, and possibly too it may be the inmost sense of the Nirvana of the Buddha : for the dissolution of our present state by Nirvana may be a reaching to some highest state beyond all notion of experience of self even, an ineffable release from our sense of existence.   Or it may be the Upanishad's absolute and unconditioned bliss which is beyond expression and beyond understanding, because it surpasses all that we can conceive of or describe as consciousness and existence.

UNSTABLES.   " Not by things unstable shall one attain That One which is stable.   By the sacrifice of momentary things I won the Eternal." (Katha Up. I. 2. 10)

UPANISAD.   Inner knowledge, that which enters into the final Truth and settles in it.
Method of Upaniṣadic Knowledge :   To listen in soul to the old voices and allow the *śruti* in the soul to respond, to vibrate, first obscurely, in answer to the Vedantic hymn of knowledge, to give the response, the echo and last to let that response gain in clarity, intensity and fullness.

UPANISHADS AND PHILOSOPHIES. The Upanishads have been the acknowledged source of numerous profound philosophies and religions that flowed from it in India like her great rivers from their Himalayan cradle fertilising the mind and life of the people and kept its soul alive through the long procession of the centuries, constantly returned to for light, never failing to give fresh illumination, a fountain of inexhaustible life-giving waters. Buddhism with all its developments was only a restatement, although from a new standpoint and with fresh terms of intellectual definition and reasoning, of one side of its experience and it carried it thus changed in form but hardly in substance over all Asia and westward towards Europe. The ideas of the Upanishads can be rediscovered in much of the thought of Pythagoras and Plato and form the profoundest part of Neo-platonism and Gnosticism with all their considerable consequences to the philosophical thinking of the West, and Sufism only repeats them in another religious language. The larger part of German metaphysics is little more in substance than an intellectual development of great realities more spiritually seen in this ancient teaching, and modern thought is rapidly absorbing them with a closer, more living and intense receptiveness which promises a revolution both in philosophical and in religious thinking ; here they are filtering in through many indirect influences, there slowly pouring through direct and open channels. There is hardly a main philosophical idea which cannot find an authority or a seed or indication in these antique writings — the speculations, according to a certain view, of thinkers who had no better past or background to their thought than a crude, barbaric, naturalistic and animistic ignorance. And even the large generalisations of Science are constantly found to apply to the truth of physical Nature formulas already discovered by the Indian sages in their original, their largest meaning in the deeper truth of the spirit.

UPANISHADS AND THE VEDA. The Rishis of the Upanishads sought to recover the lost or waning knowledge of the Veda by meditation and spiritual experience and they used the text of the ancient Mantras as a prop or an authority for their own intuitions and perceptions ; or else, the Vedic Word was a seed of thought and vision by which they recovered old truths in new forms. What they found, they expressed in other terms more intelligible in the age in which they lived.

The Upanishads claim to be a development from the Vedic knowledge, *vedānta,* repeatedly appeal to Vedic texts, regard Veda as a book of knowledge. The men who gave Vedantic knowledge are everywhere represented as teachers of the Veda.

The Upanishads take up the experience of the earlier seers and make it their starting-point for a high and profound synthesis of spiritual knowledge ; they draw together into a great harmony all that had been seen and experienced by the inspired and liberated knowers of the Eternal throughout a great and fruitful period of spiritual seeking.

The Vedantic seers renewed the Vedic truth by extricating it from its cryptic symbols and casting it into a highest and most direct and powerful language of intuition and inner experience. It was not the language of the intellect, but still it wore a form which the intellect could take hold of, translate into its own more abstract terms and convert into a starting point for an ever widening and deepening philosophic speculation and the reason's long search after a Truth original, supreme and ultimate.

UTTARĀYANA. Northern Solstice. ' By the way of the northern solstice go the souls that have sought the Spirit through holiness and knowledge and faith and askesis ; for they conquer their heavens of the Sun. There is the resting place of the breaths, there immortality casts out fear, there is the highest heavens of spirits : thence no soul returns : therefore is the wall and barrier." (Prashna Up. I. 10)

VAISVĀNARA. "He whose place is the wakefulness, who is wise of the outward ; who has seven limbs, to whom there are nineteen doors, who feels and enjoys gross objects, Vaishvanara, the Universal Male, He is the first." (Mandukya Up. 3)

VĀJIN. *Vāhano* (Vehicle) of the Gandharvas, the Horse
full of ease and plenty.
Vide Gandharvas.

VĀYU. The Life-Energy in the universe. In the light of
Surya he reveals himself as an immortal principle of existence
of which birth and death and life in the body are only particular
and external processes.

Vayu Matarisvan, the great Life-Principle, he who moves,
breathes, expands infinitely in the mother element. All things
in the universe are the movement of this mighty Life ; it is he
who has brought Agni and placed him secretly in all existence,
for him the worlds have been upbuilded that Life may move in
them, that it may act, that it may riot and enjoy.

VEDA. " Righteousness with the study and teaching of
Veda ; Truth with the study and teaching of Veda ; askesis
with the study and teaching of Veda ; self-mastery with the
study and teaching of Veda. Peace of soul with the study and
teaching of Veda. The household fires with the study and
teaching of Veda. The burnt offering with the study and
teaching of Veda. Progeny with the study and teaching of
Veda. Joy of the child's mother with the study and teaching
of Veda. Children of thy children with the study and teaching
of Veda — *these duties.* ' Truth is first ' said the truth-speaker,
the Rishi, son of Rathitara. ' Askesis is first ' said the constant
in austerity, the Rishi, son of Purushishta. ' Study and teaching
of Veda is first ' said Naka, son of Mudgala. For this too is
austerity and this too is askesis." (Taittiriya Up. I. 9)

VEDANTA. The word Vedanta is usually identified with
the strict Monism and the peculiar theory of *māyā* established
by the lofty and ascetic intellect of Shankara. But it is the
Upanishads themselves and not Shankara's writings, the text and
not the commentary, that are the authoritative Scripture of the
Vedantin. Shankara's great and temporarily satisfying as it
was, is still only one synthesis and interpretation of the Upanishads. There have been others in the past which have power-
fully influenced the rational mind and there is no reason why

there should not be a yet more perfect synthesis in the future.

Vedanta—three main schools : The individual may regard himself as eternally different from the One—*Dualism* ; or as eternally one with it, yet different — *Qualified Monism* ; or he may go back entirely in his consciousness to the pure Identity—*Monism*. These three attitudes correspond to three truths of the Brahman which are simultaneously valid and none of them entirely true without the others as its complements.

VIDYĀ AND *AVIDYĀ*. Unity is the eternal truth of things, diversity a play of the unity. The sense of unity has been therefore termed Knowledge, *Vidya*, the sense of diversity Ignorance, *avidya*. But diversity is not false except when it is divorced from the sense of its true and eternal unity.

All manifestation proceeds by the two terms, Vidya and Avidya, the consciousness of Unity and the consciousness of Multiplicity. They are the two aspects of the Maya, the formative self-conception of the Eternal.

Unity is the eternal and fundamental fact, without which all multiplicity would be unreal and an impossible illusion. The consciousness of Unity is therefore called Vidya, the Knowledge.

Multiplicity is the play or varied self-expansion of the One, shifting in its terms, divisible in its view of itself, by force of which the One occupies many centres of consciousness, inhabits many formations of energy in the individual movement. Multiplicity is implicit or explicit in unity. But the consciousness of multiplicity separated from the true knowledge in the many of their own essential oneness, — the viewpoint of the separate ego identifying itself with the divided form and the limited action, is a state of error and delusion. In man this is the form taken by the consciousness of multiplicity. Therefore it is given the name of Avidya, the Ignorance.

Brahman, the Lord, is one and all-blissful, but free from limitation by His unity ; all-powerful, He is able to conceive Himself from multiple centres in multiple forms. He is Lord of Vidya and Avidya. They are two sides of His self-conception (Maya), the twin powers of His Energy (*cit śakti*).

In the Upanishads Vidya and Avidya are spoken of as eternal in the supreme Brahman ; but this can be accepted in the sense

of the consciousness of the multiplicity and the consciousness of
the Oneness which by co-existence in the supreme self-awareness became the basis of the Manifestation ; they would there
be two sides of an eternal self-knowledge.

In the Vedantic thought of the Upanishad, — since the nature
of the Knowledge is to find the Truth and the fundamental
Truth is the One, — Vidya, Knowledge in its highest spiritual
sense, came to mean purely and trenchantly the knowledge of
the One ; Avidya, Ignorance, purely and trenchantly the knowledge of the divided many divorced, as in our world it is
divorced, from the unifying consciousness of the One Reality.
Still the later exaggerated idea of absolute separation from the
true truth of Self and Spirit, of an original illusion, of a
consciousness that can be equated with dream or with hallucina-
tion, did not at first enter into Vedantic conception of the
Ignorance.   If in the Upanishads it is declared that the man
who lives and moves within the Ignorance, wanders about
stumbling like a blind man led by the blind and returns ever to
the net of Death which is spread wide for him, it is also affirmed
elsewhere in the Upanishads that he who follows after the
Knowledge only, enters as if into a blinder darkness than he
who follows after the Ignorance and that the man who knows
Brahman as both the Ignorance and the Knowledge, as both the
One and the Many, as both the Becoming and the Non-
becoming, crosses by the Ignorance, by the experience of the
Multiplicity, beyond death and by the Knowledge takes possession of Immortality.   For the Self-existent has really become
these many existences ; the Upanishad can say to the Divine
Being, in all solemnity and with no thought to mislead, " Thou
art this old man walking with his staff, yonder boy and girl,
this blue-winged bird, that red of eye." not " Thou seemest to
be these things " to the self-deluding mind of the Ignorance.
The status of becoming is inferior to the status of Being, but
still it is the Being that becomes all that is in the universe.

The purpose of the Lord in the world cannot be fulfilled by
following Vidya alone or Avidya alone.

Those who are devoted entirely to the principle of multiplicity and division and take their orientation away from oneness
enter into a blind darkness of Ignorance.   For this tendency is

one of increasing contraction and limitation, disaggregation of the gains of knowledge and greater and greater subjection to the mechanical necessities of Prakriti and finally to her separative and self-destructive forces. To turn away from the progression towards Oneness is to turn away from existence and from light.

Those who are devoted entirely to the principle of indiscriminate Unity and seek to put away from them the integrality of the Brahman, also put away from them knowledge and completeness and enter as if into a greater darkness. They enter into some special state and accept it for the whole, mistaking exclusion in consciousness for transcendence in consciousness. They ignore by choice of knowledge, as the others are ignorant by compulsion of error. Knowing all to transcend all is the right path of Vidya.

Although a higher state than the other, this supreme Night is termed a greater darkness, because the lower is one of the chaos from which reconstitution is always possible, the higher is a conception of Void or Asat, an attachment to non-existence of Self from which it is more difficult to return to fulfilment of Self.

Pursued with a less entire attachment the paths of Vidya and Avidya have each their legitimate gains for the human soul, but neither of these are the full and perfect thing undertaken by the individual in the manifestation.

By Vidya one may attain to the state of the silent Brahman or the Akshara Purusha regarding the universe without actively participating in it or to His self-absorbed state of Chit in Sat from which the universe proceeds and towards which it returns. Both these states are conditions of serenity, plenitude, freedom from the confusions and sufferings of the world.

But the highest goal of man is neither fulfilment in the movement as a separate individual nor in the Silence separated from the movement, but in the Uttama Purusha, the Lord, He who went abroad and upholds in Himself both the Kshara and the Akshara as modes of His being. The self of man, the Jivatman, is here in order to realise in the individual and for the universe that one highest Self of all. The ego created by Avidya is a necessary mechanism for affirming individuality in the universal as a starting point for this supreme achievement.

By Avidya one may attain to a sort of fullness of power, joy, world-knowledge, largeness of being, which is that of the Titans or of the Gods, of Indra, of Prajapati. This is gained in the path of self-enlargement by an ample acceptance of the multiplicity in all its possibilities and a constant enrichment of the individual by all the materials that the universe can pour into him. But this also is not the goal of man ; for though it brings transcendence of the ordinary human limits, it does not bring the divine transcendence of the universe in the Lord of the universe. One transcends confusion of Ignorance, but not limitation of Knowledge, — transcends death of the body, but not limitation of being, — transcends subjection to sorrow, but not subjection of joy, — transcends the lower Prakriti, but not the higher. To gain the real freedom and the perfect Immortality one would have to descend again to all that had been rejected and make the right use of death, sorrow and ignorance.

The real knowledge is that which perceives Brahman in His integrality and does not follow eagerly after one consciousness rather than another, is no more attached to Vidya than to Avidya.

VIJÑĀNA: The original comprehensive consciousness which holds an image of things in its essence, totality and parts and properties ; it is the original, spontaneous, true and complete view of it which belongs properly to the supermind and of which mind has only a shadow in the highest operations of the comprehensive intellect.

The causal Idea (supramental Real-Idea), or supramental Knowledge-Will. It is the causal Idea which, by supporting and secretly guiding the confused activities of the Mind, Life and Body, ensures and compels the right arrangement of the universe. It is called in the Veda the Truth because it represents by direct vision the truth of things both inclusive and independent of their appearances ; the Right or Law, because, containing in itself the effective power of Cit, it works out all things according to their nature with a perfect knowledge and prevision ; the Vast, because it is of the nature of an infinite cosmic Intelligence comprehensive of all particular activities.

Vijnana as the Truth, leads the divided consciousness back to the One. It also sees the truth of things in the multiplicity. Vijnana is the divine counterpart of the lower divided intelligence.

Knowledge by discrimination.

The *Vijnāna* or gnosis is not only truth but truth-power, it is the very working of the infinite and divine nature ; it is the divine knowledge one with the divine will in the force and delight of a spontaneous and luminous and inevitable self-fulfilment. By the gnosis, then, we change our human into a divine nature.

Three Powers of Vijnāna : To the envisaging mind there are three powers of the Vijnana. Its supreme power knows and receives into it from above all the infinite existence, consciousness and bliss of the Ishvara ; it is in its highest height the absolute knowledge and the force of eternal Sachchidananda. Its second power concentrates the Infinite into a dense luminous consciousness, *caitanyaghana* or *cidghana,* the seed-state of the divine consciousness in which are contained living and concrete all the immutable principles of the divine being and all the inviolable truths of the divine conscious-idea and nature. Its third power brings or looses out these things by the effective ideation, vision, authentic identities of the divine knowledge, movement of the divine will-force, vibration of the divine delight-intensities into a universal harmony, an illimitable diversity, a manifold rhythm of their powers, forms and interplay of living consequences.

The mental Purusha rising into the *vijnānamaya* must ascend into these three powers. It must turn by conversion of its movements into the movements of the gnosis, its mental perception, ideation, will, pleasure into radiances of the divine knowledge, pulsations of the divine will-force, waves and floods of the divine delight-seas. It must convert its conscious stuff of mental nature into the *cidghana* or dense luminous consciousness. It must transform its conscious substance into a gnostic self or Truth-self of infinite Sachchidananda. These three movements are described in the Isha Upanishad, the first as *vyūha,* the marshalling of the rays of the Sun of gnosis in the order of the Truth-consciousness, the second as *samūha,*

the gathering together of the rays into the body of the Sun of
gnosis, the third as the vision of that Sun's fairest form of all
in which the soul most intimately possesses its oneness with the
infinite Purusha.*   The Supreme above, in him, around, everywhere and the soul dwelling in the Supreme and one with it,
— the infinite power and truth of the Divine concentrated in
his own concentrated luminous soul nature, — a radiant activity
of the divine knowledge, will and joy perfect in the natural
action of the Prakriti, — this is the fundamental experience of
the mental being transformed and fulfilled and sublimated in
the perfection of the gnosis.

   Vijñāna and Buddhi :   One error of intellect-bounded thinkers
takes *vijñāna* as synonymous with the other Indian term *buddhi*
and the *buddhi* as synonymous with the reason, the discerning
intellect, the logical intelligence.   The systems that accept this
significance, pass at once from a plane of pure intellect to a
plane of pure spirit.   No intermediate power is recognised, no
diviner action of knowledge than the pure reason is admitted ;
the limited human means for facing truth is taken for the
highest possible dynamics of consciousness, its topmost force and
original movement.   An opposite error, a misconception of the
mystics identifies *vijñāna* with the consciousness of the Infinite
free from all ideation or else ideation packed into one essence
of thought, lost to other dynamic action in the single and
invariable idea of the One.   This is the *caitanyaghana* of the
Upanishad and is one movement or rather one thread of the
many-aspected movement of the gnosis.   The gnosis, the Vijnana
is not only this concentrated consciousness of the infinite
Essence ; it is also and at the same time an infinite knowledge
of the myriad play of the Infinite.   It contains all ideation (not
mental but supramental), but it is not limited by ideation, for

---

* *Surya, vyuha rasmin samuha, tejo yat te rupam kalyanataman tat te
pasyami, yo'savasau pursah so'hamasmi.*   The Veda describes the Vijnana
plane as *rtam, satyam, brhat,* the Right, Truth, Vast, the same triple idea
differently expressed.   Ritam is the action of the divine knowledge, will
and joy in the lines of the truth, the play of the Truth-consciousness.
Satyam is the truth of being which so acts, the dynamic essence of the
Truth-consciousness.   Brihat is the infinity of Sachchidananda out of which
the other two proceed and in which they are founded.

it far exceeds all ideative movement. Nor is the gnostic ideation in its character an intellectual thinking; it is not what we call the reason, not a concentrated intelligence. For the reason is mental in its methods, mental in its acquisitions, mental in its basis, but the ideative method of the gnosis is self-luminous, supramental, its yield of thought-light spontaneous, not proceeding by acquisition, its thought-basis a rendering of conscious identities, nor a translation of the impressions born of indirect contacts. There is a relation and even a sort of broken identity between the two forms of thought; for one proceeds covertly from other. Mind is born from that which is beyond mind. But they act on different planes and reverse each other's process.

VIJNĀNAM BRAHMA. " He knew Knowledge for the Eternal. For from Knowledge alone, it appears, are these creatures born and being born they live by Knowledge and to Knowledge they go hence and return." (Taittiriya Up. III. 5)

VIJNĀNAMAYA ĀTMA. " There is yet a second and inner self which is other than this which is of Mind and is made of Knowledge. And the Self of Knowledge fills the Self of Mind. Now the Knowledge Self is made in the image of a man; according as is the human image of the other, so is it in the image of the man. Faith is the head of him, Law is his right side, Truth is his left side ; Yoga is his spirit which is the self of him ; Mahas is his lower member whereon he rests abidingly." (Taittiriya Up. II. 4)

" Knowledge spreads the feast of sacrifice and knowledge spreads also the feast of works ; all the gods offer adoration to him as to Brahman and the Elder of the Universe. For if one worship Brahman as the knowledge and if one swerve not from it, neither falter, then he casts sin from him in this body and tastes all desire. And this Self of Knowledge is the soul in the body to the former one which was of Mind." (Taittiriya Up. II. 5)

VIRĀT. Brahman manifest in the Universe of gross Matter as the Ruler, Guide, Self and Helper.

VYĀHRITIS. " Words of His naming. Bhur, Bhuvar and Suvar, these are the three Words of His naming. Verily, the Rishi Mahachamasya made known a fourth to these, which is Mahas. It is Brahman, it is the Self, and the other gods are his members. Bhur, it is this world ; Bhuvar, it is the sky ; Suvar, it is the other world ; but Mahas is the Sun. By the Sun all these worlds increase and prosper. Bhur, it is the Fire ; Bhuvar, it is Air ; Suvar it is the Sun ; but Mahas is the Moon. By the Moon all these lights of heaven increase and prosper. Bhur, it is the hymns of the Rigveda ; Bhuvar, it is the hymns of the Sama ; Suvar, it is the hymns of the Yajur; but Mahas is the Eternal. By the Eternal all these Vedas increase and prosper. Bhur, it is the main breath ; Bhuvar, it is the lower breath ; Suvar, it is the breath pervasor ; but Mahas is food. By food all these breaths increase and prosper. These are the four and they are fourfold ; — four Words of His naming and each is four again. He who knows these knows the Eternal, and to him all the Gods carry the offering." (Taittiriya Up. I. 5)

VYĀKARANA. The Vedantic writers dwelt deeply| and curiously on the innate and on the concealed meaning of words ; *vyākaraṇa,* always considered essential to the interpretation of the Vedas, they used not merely as scholars, but much more as intuitive thinkers. It was not only the actual etymological sense or the actual sense in use but the suggestions of the sound and syllables of the words which attracted them ; for they found that by dwelling on them new and deep truths arose into their understandings.

WISE ONE. " The Wise One is not born, neither does he die : he came not from anywhere, neither is he anyone : he is unborn, he is ever-lasting, he is ancient and sempiternal : he is not slain in the slaying of the body. If the slayer think that he slays, if the slain think that he is slain, both of these have not the knowledge. This slays not, neither is He slain." (Katha Up. I. 2. 18, 19)

WORK. " Brahman grows by his energy at work, and then from Him is Matter born, and out of Matter life, and mind and truth and the worlds, and in works immortality." (Mundaka Up. I. 1. 8)

WORKS AND KNOWLEDGE. The opposition between works and knowledge exists as long as work and knowledge are only of the egoistic mental character.

" This is That, the Truth of things : works which the sages beheld in the Mantras were in the Treta manifoldly extended. Works do ye perform religiously with one passion for the Truth ; this is your road to the heaven of Good deeds." (Mundaka Up. I. 2. 1)

" He does works by Om who has the knowledge, and he also who has it not ; but these are diverse, the Knowledge and the Ignorance. Whatsoever work one does with knowledge, with faith and with the secret of Vedas, it becomes to him more virile and mighty." (Chhandogya Up. I. 1. 10)

WORLD. In the Vedantic conception a world is only a condition of conscious being organised in the terms of the seven constituent principles of manifested existence.

The worlds of which the Upanishad speaks are essentially soul-conditions and not geographical divisions of the cosmos. This material universe is itself only existence as we see it when the soul dwells on the plane of material movement and experience in which the spirit involves itself in form, and therefore all the framework of things in which it moves by the life and which it embraces by the consciousness is determined by the principle of infinite division and aggregation proper to Matter, to substance of form. This becomes then its world or vision of things. And to whatever soul-condition it climbs, its vision of things will change and correspond to that condition, and in that framework it will move in its living and embrace it in its consciousness. These are the worlds of the ancient tradition.

WORLD-VIEW. The Upanishads do not deny life, but hold that the world is a manifestation of the Eternal, of Brahman, all here is Brahman, all is in the Spirit and the Spirit is in all, the self-existent Spirit has become all these things and creatures ; life too is Brahman, the life-force is the very basis of our

existence, the life-spirit, Vayu, is the manifest and evident
Eternal *pratyakṣam brahma*. But it affirmed that the present
way of existence of man is not the highest of the whole : his
outward mind and life are not all his being ; to be fulfilled and
perfect he has to grow out of his physical and mental ignorance
into spiritual self-knowledge.

YAMA. Lord of death, also the master of the Law in the
world he is therefore the child of the Sun, luminous Master of
Truth from which the Law is born.
Yama is the knower and keeper of the cosmic Law through
which the soul has to rise by death and life to the freedom of
Immortality.

YOGIC ACTION. The status of an inner passivity and an
outer action independent of each other is a state of entire spiritual freedom. The Yogin even in acting does no actions, for
it is not he, but universal Nature directed by the Lord of Nature
which is at work. He is not bound by his works, nor do they
leave any after-effects or consequences in his mind, nor cling to
or leave any mark on his soul (*na karma lipyate nare*) ; they
vanish and are dissolved by their very execution and leave the
immutable self unaffected and the soul unmodified.

YOGIC STATE. " When the five senses cease and are at rest
and the mind rests with them and the higher mind ceases from
its workings, that is the highest state, say thinkers.
The state unperturbed when the senses are imprisoned in the
mind, of this they say ' It is Yoga '. Then man becomes very
vigilant, for Yoga is the birth of things and their ending."
(Katha Up. II. 3. 10-11)

THE LIFE DIVINE
by Sri Aurobindo
$20.00; paper; 1070 pp.; $25.00; hardbound

The Life Divine is Sri Aurobindo's major philosophical
exposition, spanning more than a thousand pages
and integrating the major spiritual directions of
mankind into a coherent picture of the growth of
the spiritual essence of man through diverse
methods, philosophies and spiritual practices.
Within the scope of the book Sri Aurobindo grants
us a view of the panorama of the evolution of
man within the framework of the development
of the universe around us, exploring all the
major questions which have occupied men
from the first dawns of human aspiration to
the challenges confronting us today.

BASES OF YOGA
by Sri Aurobindo
$2.95; 108 pp.; paper

Bases of Yoga is a concise handbook of yoga,
written to aid the seeker wishing to start
down the path of spiritual practice, and
giving insight and clues which are
invaluable to the sincere spiritual aspirant
of any path.

PRAYERS AND MEDITATIONS
by The Mother
$12.95; paper; 380 pp.; $15.95; hardbound

Prayers and meditations is the outpouring of
spiritual energy of Sri Aurobindo's co-worker, the
Mother of the Sri Aurobindo Ashram. This book
has the power to express the universal spiritual
aspiration of humanity and brings the force of
dedication and spiritual focus to the reader. It is
simple, direct and touching. It is a valuable aid to
sadhana for all regardless of the particular teaching that you follow.

VEDIC SYMBOLISM

by Sri Aurobindo
compiled by Sri. M.P. Pandit

$6.95; 122 pp.; paper; ISBN: 0-941524-30-2

The value of the Rig Veda as a guidebook to spiritual
practice has been obscured due to the heavy veil of
symbols used by the Rishis to hide their meaning
from the uninitiated. Sri Aurobindo, through many
years of research and sadhana, was able to unlock the
secret of the veda and give us the key to the symbolic
system of the Vedic Rishis.

"Vedic Symbolism" introduces the major vedic concepts and reveals their esoteric sense.
Sri Aurobindo's work has given the study of the Rig Veda new relevance and has made the
imagery of the Veda reveal its hidden meaning. It is an important contribution to the vedic
literature.

LIVING WITHIN:
Yoga Approach to Psychological Health and Growth

by Sri Aurobindo and the Mother
Compiled with an introduction by Dr. A.S. Dalal

$6.95; 179 pp.; paper; ISBN: 0-941524-22-1

Western psychotherapy and personal growth process has gained considerably from the
experience acquired within Eastern traditions. Dr. A.S. Dalal has lived and worked in both
the world of Western mental health and the world of Eastern spiritual discipline. He draws
on the deep insights of Sri Aurobindo and the Mother to locate the origins and solutions to
ordinary problems in living as well as psychotherapy. This is a highly recommended
introduction for both the psychological professional and the individual interested in living
a life of health and balance.

OTHER TITLES BY SRI AUROBINDO:

Bases of Yoga	p	2.95
Essays on the Gita	p	16.50
	hb	18.95
Hymns to the Mystic Fire	p	22.50
Isha Upanishad	p	3.95
Life Divine	p	20.00
	hb	25.00
Lights on Yoga	p	2.50
Living Within	p	6.95
Message of the Gita w. text	p	8.95
The Mother	p	1.50
Practical Guide to Integral Yoga	p	7.95
Problem of Rebirth	p	7.95
Savitri: Legend & Symbol	p	16.00
	hb	21.95
Secret of the Veda	p	15.00
	hb	18.00
Synthesis of Yoga	p	16.00
	hb	19.50
Upanishads	p	16.50
Vedic Symbolism	p	6.95

available from your local bookseller or

LOTUS LIGHT PUBLICATIONS
P.O. Box 2, Wilmot, WI 53192 U.S.A.
(414) 862-2395